Luis Coloma

Twayne's World Authors Series
Spanish Literature

Janet Pérez, Editor
Texas Tech University

TWAS 793

LUIS COLOMA
(c. 1890)
Reprinted from *Illustración Española y Americana*, Año XXXV, Número XXXIII, Madrid, September 8, 1891. Courtesy of the University of Michigan Library.

Luis Coloma

By Gerard Flynn

University of Wisconsin–Milwaukee

Twayne Publishers

A Division of G.K. Hall & Co. • Boston

Luis Coloma

Gerard Flynn

Copyright 1987 by G.K. Hall & Co.
All rights reserved.
Published by Twayne Publishers
A Division of G.K. Hall & Co.
70 Lincoln Street
Boston, Massachusetts   02111

Copyediting supervised by Lewis DeSimone
Book production by John Amburg
Book design by Barbara Anderson

Typeset in 11 pt Garamond
by Compset, Inc.

Printed on permanent/durable acid-free paper
and bound in the United States of America

Library of Congress Cataloging in Publication Data

Flynn, Gerard C.
  Luis Coloma.

  (Twayne's world authors series ; TWAS 793.
Spanish literature)
  Bibliography: p.
  Includes index.
  1. Coloma, Luis, 1851–1915—Criticism and
interpretation. I. Title. II. Series: Twayne's
world authors series ; TWAS 793.   Spanish
literature.
PQ6605.O5Z67   1987   863'.5   87-13867
ISBN 0-8057-6647-2 (alk. paper)

Contents

About the Author

Gerard Flynn is professor of Spanish at the University of Wisconsin–Milwaukee. He has published three volumes in Twayne's World Authors Series, *Sor Juana Inés de la Cruz, Manuel Tamayo y Baus,* and *Manuel Bretón de los Herreros,* as well as a students' edition of Pío Baroja's *El árbol de la ciencia.* He has also published articles on various literary subjects in professional journals.

Preface

The purpose of this book is to introduce the reader to the Spanish novelist Luis Coloma (1851–1915). The first chapter emphasizes his biography; the following chapters, his stories, novels, and novelistic histories and biographies. For insights into his life I have relied primarily on the biographies and articles of Father Rafael Hornedo, the biography of Doña Emilia Pardo Bazán, and the few editions of Coloma's letters. Hornedo's study of his fellow Jesuit, published as a favorable introduction to Coloma's *Complete Works,* is thorough.

Since the past criticism of Coloma has often been divided between critics who share his extremely traditionalist views and critics who do not, literary analysis has been neglected amid a multitude of political, social, and religious preferences. Some noteworthy exceptions in this atmosphere of bias are the brief studies of Federico Balart, Emilio Bobadilla, Brian Dendle, Javier Herrero, Doña Emilia Pardo Bazán, and the *tour de poésie* of Don Juan Valera. One must add to this list the profound introduction of Rubén Benítez to the 1975 edition of Coloma's *Bagatelles.*[1]

I have included two English translations from Coloma in appendixes 1 and 2. The first is a letter he wrote to the journalist Luis Alfonso during the *Bagatelles* scandal of March–April 1891, which gives a faithful impression of Coloma the moralist, the "missionary-novelist" as he called himself, defending the right and the holy. The second translation is from book 2, chapter 2 of *Bagatelles,* where the degenerate Spanish grandee, Uncle Frasquito, appears prior to his meeting the lapsed Mason, Jacobo Sabadell. Here the "missionary-novelist" has forgotten himself and created a caricature out of pure aesthetic joy. Coloma's literary accomplishment depends above all on creations like Uncle Frasquito and his restoration of history.

Coloma wrote forty-one stories, two novels, six historical biographies, an academy speech, and two works we may call devotional. I have discussed all of them at length in the present volume, except the stories, of which I have included five. These works are readily accessible in the fourth edition of the *Obras completas.*[2]

I should draw the reader's attention to chapter 7, which contains three significant short works of Father Luis Coloma, S.J. His *Spiritual*

Exercises for the young king Alfonso XIII are as Jansenistic as anything
to be found in seventeenth-century France. His history of the relics of
St. Francis Borgia, whose body never found a permanent resting place,
resembles the history of his own Jesuit order and himself and accounts
in a way for his siege mentality in the face of modern revolution. And
his Academy speech, written in honor of Father José Francisco de Isla,
S.J., the great satirist of the eighteenth century, reveals the inner spirit
of Luis Coloma, the Jesuit satirist of the nineteenth century. His religious order was his bride.

The Selected Bibliography records the comments of many critics of
Coloma; the reader will find other comments in the text of the present
book and in the Notes and References. All the translations from Coloma's stories, novels, and other prose are mine; they cannot be found
elsewhere. With the exception of *Bagatelles* and *Boy* most of the quo-
tations in this book are taken from the fourth edition of the *Obras
completas,* cited in the text as *OC.* For *Pequeñeces* (Bagatelles) I have used
the 1975 edition of Rubén Benítez, and for *Boy* the Editorial Porrúa
edition of 1966.[3] There is, lastly, a list of English translations in the
Selected Bibliography.

I owe several debts of gratitude to my editor, Professor Janet Pérez,
for her loyal criticism; to my colleague, Professor Pierre Ullman, for
his careful correction of the manuscript; and to Miss Jane Koenig, for
her patient typing of these pages. I owe special thanks to my wife,
Geraldine, for her encouragement.

Gerard Flynn

University of Wisconsin–Milwaukee

Chronology

1851 9 January, Luis Coloma born in Jerez de la Frontera, Andalusia.

1868 15 June, finishes his secondary education. 18 September, The Glorious Revolution, expelling the Bourbon dynasty from Spain, exerts a lifelong effect on the traditionalist, Luis Coloma: it is frequently mentioned in his stories, novels, and histories.

1868–1873 Studies law in Seville, works for the restoration of the Bourbon monarchy, and becomes friendly with the well-known woman novelist, Fernán Caballero. She guides his first literary efforts, which are *costumbrista* (local color).

1872 September–October, "the mysterious event": he suffers a bullet wound in the chest, the secret of which he carries to the grave.

1874 22 October, enters the novitiate of the Society of Jesus in Poyanne, France, where the exiled Jesuits maintain their seminary. Maintains correspondence with Caballero until her death in 1877.

1884 February, his story, "A Miracle," appears in the *Sacred Heart Messenger,* a monthly magazine he helps to edit. His works appear in serial form in the *Messenger* before publication as books.

1888 February, suffers a severe liver attack and headaches. He is plagued by ill health all his life.

1890 *Pequeñeces* published in serial form, in the *Messenger,* attracting little attention.

1891 March–April, publication of *Pequeñeces* in book form, the first of many printings, startles the reading public. The *Pequeñeces* affair has been called the *algarada* (war cry).

1895 *Retratos de antaño* evokes the atmosphere of eighteenth-century France.

1895–1896   Coloma's other novel, his personal favorite, *Boy*, published serially in the *Messenger*, but the Jesuit superiors forbid its publication after chapter 11. The reason for their ban has never been disclosed.

1895–1911   Coloma writes novelistic histories and biographies rather than novels.

1898   *La reina mártir*, the story of Mary Stuart.

1903–1907   *Jeromín*, the story of Don John of Austria.

1907–1910   *Recuerdos de Fernán Caballero*, setting down Coloma's recollections of his old friend.

1908   6 December, enters the Royal Academy of Language and delivers his speech on "The Author of Fray Gerundio," P. José Francisco de Isla.

1910   *Boy*. Coloma writes to a friend: "This mutilated and limited *Boy* is but a pale reflection of the original."

1911   *Fray Francisco*, the story of Cardinal Cisneros. Coloma does not live to complete the second half.

1911–1915   Ill health and obscurity.

1915   10 June, Coloma dies on the vigil of the Feast of the Sacred Heart.

Chapter One

The Nineteenth-Century Jesuit Priest

Luis Coloma and Thomas à Kempis

To understand Luis Coloma one must first read Thomas à Kempis's *Imitation of Christ*, written by a monk of the fifteenth century for other monks as a guide to the religious life. "The Kempis," as Coloma used to call this book, was his favorite reading. He quotes from it in several of his didactic stories:

You must act in all your thoughts and deeds as if you were to die the next moment. (*OC*, 141)

Not because they praise you are you better, nor more vile because they vituperate you. (*OC*, 306, 1259)

Neither should you inquire about nor discuss the merits of the saints, which one is more holy or greater in the kingdom of heaven. Much more pleasing to God is he who thinks about the gravity of his sins and paucity of his virtue and how far he is from the saints' perfection. . . . (*OC*, 410)

Think of death and you will be saved. . . . (*OC*, 1011)

A sense of one's own lowliness, the contemplation of death and salvation, and a detachment from worldly goods and fame—these were the doctrines that Kempis preached to his fellow monks, who had withdrawn from the world; and these were also the doctrines that Father Luis Coloma preached, not to the monks of the nineteenth century, but to Spaniards of all classes. On one occasion he emphasized the *desengaño* of Kempis (*OC*, 1268), which may be translated as "the realization of the truth" or "disillusionment with the world," for to realize the truth is to experience worldly disillusion.

1

Applying his religious beliefs to art, Coloma looked upon the novel as a superstructure raised in the public square for preaching to the faithful, and the novelist himself as a missionary. In days gone by a priest might deliver a sermon from a church pulpit or special platform, but in the 1880s and 1890s such a sermon was no longer adequate, not when, as Coloma saw it, all of society was endangered and the lesson to be presented was devastating.[1] This attitude will explain Coloma's self-confidence and comparative serenity throughout the bitter controversy in 1891 over his novel *Pequeñeces* (Bagatelles), which preached traditional values, excoriated the liberals and Masons, and made fun of certain elements of the aristocracy. The tumult caused was unanticipated, but, after all, he was preaching the gospel as his station in life demanded. This attitude, moreover, seems to explain his silent pain and wonderment during the fifteen year suppression (1895 to 1910) of his novel *Boy* by the superiors of the Jesuit order, for as a novelist without a novel he was a priest without a pulpit!

Early Life: 1851–74

Luis Coloma was born in Jerez de la Frontera, in the province of Andalusia, on 9 January 1851. His father, Ramón Coloma, was a medical doctor of some renown who had gone to Jerez in 1834 to minister to the victims of cholera there. Remaining in Jerez, he raised a large family by two wives, the second of whom was Luis Coloma's mother. The Coloma family was well situated in the society of Jerez; as a young boy Luis attended the school of Don José del Rincón, to whom the most prominent families sent their children. He must have acquired a certain social ease in this school and at home, for all his life he enjoyed the intimacy of persons of the upper class, especially the aristocracy. For example, one of his histories, published later in life, has a dedication to the Most Excellent Duke of Luna, beginning with these words: "My dear Joey: it has been twenty years now that I started to sketch in *Portraits of Yore* the grave and severe figure of your (*tú*) grandmother, the duchess of Villahermosa. . . ." This familiarity with the aristocracy will account for the genuineness of many scenes in Coloma's most famous work, *Bagatelles*, which many of his contemporaries preferred to other novels concerning the aristocracy.[2]

As a boy of thirteen, Luis attended a naval college, but after one semester he lost interest in a maritime career. In the novel *Boy*, Xavier, count of Baza, is a young naval officer, and the knowledge of naval custom displayed in this story probably comes from this phase of Coloma's life. The years 1864–68 brought a series of reforms to Spanish secondary education, with the result that Coloma took a year more than usual to complete his studies. He seems to have been an ordinary student at the Institute in Jerez, although he did well in French; this attraction to France was to last all his life, for the aristocratic figures of his novels and histories are either Frenchmen or Spaniards who frequently wear French garb, eat French food, drop French phrases, and travel to France for extended visits. Coloma will even pun in French (see *OC*, 1462). This attraction, however, was ambivalent, since Paris, the fairest of all cities, was also the mother of vice, the latter-day Babylonia; following the example of Louis Veuillot, Coloma calls Paris "the university of the seven capital sins" (see *OC*, 1211).[3]

One statistic, the rate of illiteracy, is important for an understanding of Luis Coloma. In the 1860s and 1870s more than 70 percent of Spanish citizens could not read or write, and the figures ran higher in Andalusia, so that a man like Coloma, who had studied Greek, French, English, law, Latin, philosophy, and theology, belonged to a select group of Spaniards. Thus, perhaps unaware, he had a peculiar ethical code: in his writings he clearly shows a preference for the upper classes. He may castigate or even flog the Madrid aristocracy in his stories, with *Bagatelles* becoming "the pillory of the Restoration," but he is really trying to set his own house in order. His code is always that of Christian and gentleman, the two being inseparable, and in his chapters on the duke of Villahermosa (in *Portraits of Yore* and *The Marquis de Mora*) the code of gentlemanliness almost takes precedence over Christian behavior. Furthermore, Luis Coloma's vision of personal salvation has much to do with social position. In his novels and stories one frequently encounters the idea that the poor and well-to-do exist for each other, the former to practice Christian resignation in the face of adversity, and the latter, witnessing their neighbors' hardship, to practice charity, giving freely of their wealth to the poor. Coloma was by no means alone in this attitude; Manuel Tamayo y Baus (1829–98), for example, displays the same mentality in his melodramas.

The day of 19 September 1868 must have been the most memorable in the life of Luis Coloma, for it became the one he most frequently alluded to in his writings. He had just traveled to Seville to enroll in the university there and had taken lodging in the house at 34 Zaragoza Street, where his brother José was residing, when news came that generals Prim and Serrano and Rear Admiral Topete had rebelled against the government of Isabel II. Thus began the famous Revolution of September 1868. Coloma returned immediately to his home in Jerez, to find some most unwelcome innovations of the revolutionary junta there: the prohibition of bell tolling for the dead, the closing of churches not destined for parish use, and the establishment of revolutionary clubs in convents. For a man whose political philosophy is summed up in the words "the altar and the throne," these deeds must have seemed shocking.[4] In any case, Coloma always speaks of revolutionaries with disgust, even when he applies the word to rebellious feudal lords disrupting the realm of Henry IV (1425–74). The reason is simple: revolutionaries for Coloma are traitors.

Coloma's residence at the University of Seville coincided with rapid changes in government, which make it difficult to trace his scholastic record there. The revolutionary government of 1868–70 legislated egalitarian reforms in the universities that resulted in student absenteeism and the elimination of grades such as outstanding, high pass, pass, and fail, the only grades being pass and not pass. The government of Amadeo I, the Italian prince who ruled Spain from 1870 to 1873, attempted to restore the old system, but the federal republic of 1873 and 1874 returned to the egalitarian platform. Coloma appears to have been a good though not distinguished law student. At this time his father became gravely ill, and his beloved brother José, scarcely older than he, died in Cuba of yellow fever. José had preceded him in law school and was a government attorney.

During his years at school, Coloma read widely on many subjects, but works of a devotional or moralizing cast, such as those of the Spaniard Jaime Balmes and the Frenchman Louis Veuillot, held special interest for him. A work he mentions almost as much as "The Kempis" was Silvio Pellico's *My Years in Prison,* which he read in the French translation of De Latour.[5] One can readily understand his attraction to Pellico (1789–1854), the Italian patriot whose trust in divine providence guided him through ten horrible years as a political prisoner. Pellico's style differs radically from Coloma's because he does not, in his own words, "blend in even a bit of that satirical coloring so commonly found in moralists,"[6] but his resignation to God's plan in history is the same. In Coloma's novel, *Boy,* Xavier's words "Bind me, Lord, and have mercy on me," could have been written by Pellico in his Spielberg prison.[7] And one anecdote of Pellico might well have been the inspiration, hidden in the recesses of Coloma's mind but never forgotten, for *Bagatelles.* While at Spielberg, Pellico tells us that his

Bible gathered dust and that he was so unhappy he began to calumniate his fellowmen and even his creator. He looked at everything with the wisdom of the cynics. Then one day his jailer told him that whenever he read that "doggone book" (*libraco*) he did not seem so melancholy. So he took the book, dusted it, opened it at random, and chanced upon the following lines: "It is impossible that scandals not happen: but woe is he through whose fault they come. Better it were for him that they put a millstone round his neck and cast him into the sea than that he scandalize one of these my little ones." For the religious mind of Luis Coloma, Pellico's experience was no mere chance nor was there chance in his own reading about it. Surely providence was at work here. Scandal, the sin by which one person leads another into evil is never a bagatelle, though others may treat it so; this is the theme of Coloma's novel, *Bagatelles*.

During the years prior to 1874 Coloma also read the literature of two famous Spanish ladies, Cecilia Böhl de Faber (1796–1877), marchioness of Arco Hermoso, whose pen name was Fernán Caballero, and the Cuban-Spanish author Tula, Gertrudis Gómez de Avellaneda (1814–73). He came to know both these women personally, especially Fernán Caballero, whose *costumbrismo* (local color) and moralizing stories became the model for his first literary efforts. Later in life, when almost sixty years of age, he published *Memories of Fernán Caballero,* a book recalling this kindly friend of his youth.

One event of Coloma's life is so vaguely known that his principal biographer has called it "the mysterious event."[8] In the fall of 1872, apparently in late September or early October, Coloma lay gravely ill with a bullet wound in his chest. Several theories have been advanced concerning the origin of the wound: the young Luis Coloma attempted suicide; or he fought in a duel; or he became the victim of a love affair. One Andalusian writer, Genaro Cavestany, arguing for a love affair, changed the nature of the wound to a knife stab.[9] Coloma's most searching biographer, Rafael Hornedo, has concluded that the bullet was accidentally discharged while Coloma was cleaning a weapon.[10] Be that as it may, Father Luis Coloma apparently never discussed the issue with anyone and carried the mystery of his chest wound to the grave.

The years of Coloma's early manhood, 1868–74, saw profound changes in Spanish politics: the exiling of Queen Isabel II in 1868; "Spain without a Monarch" (1868–70);[11] the short-lived dynasty of the Italian "intruder," Amadeo I (1870–73); the first republic; the restoration of the Bourbon dynasty through Queen Isabel's son, Alfonso

XII, in 1875; and the Carlist civil war. Throughout these changes the young Luis Coloma was a staunch supporter of Alfonso. On one occasion Fernán Caballero asked him to take care of some political documents; he did not know he was under police surveillance at the time, and his action resulted in a search of his residence. This episode, which was never forgotten, served him some twenty years later in one scene of *Bagatelles*, where the police make a thorough search of the palace of Countess Currita Albornoz. The scandalous Currita insists on a legal detail, demanding "the writ of the governor, notarized by the judge, the only authority under existing law who can authorize such an outrage."[12]

Politics plays a broad role in all of Coloma's literature, whether he is writing about Henry IV, the Catholic monarchs and Cardinal Cisneros in the fifteenth century, Mary Stuart and Don John of Austria in the sixteenth century, the French crown in the eighteenth century, or the Spanish crown in the nineteenth century. In some chapter or paragraph he always favors traditionalism, which perceives the altar and throne as the two cornerstones of society, and he always opposes revolution, the doctrine of impious men.

The Jesuit Priest

Some writers have argued that Coloma's decision to enter the Jesuit order was prompted by "the mysterious event" described above, the bullet wound and providential sparing of his life. Such writers can point to the religious conversion of another novelist, Pedro Antonio de Alarcón (1833–91) to gain credence for their argument.[13] On the other hand, Coloma's coreligionists see no causal connection between the act of violence and the act of religion; their chronology is merely accidental. In the absence of documentary evidence, one can only say that Coloma always considered his priesthood and role as a Jesuit a vocation, a special act of divine providence that he necessarily followed. Given this argument, it seems of little moment whether the almighty called him through the violence of a bullet wound, the contemplation of a rosebud in June,[14] or the immediate apprehension of joy in being.[15] As Luis Coloma himself put it, "God writes straight with twisted lines."

Coloma entered the Society of Jesus, or "the Company," as it is called in Spanish, on 5 October 1874. Since the Jesuits were exiled from Spain at the time, he spent the two years of his novitiate at the Chateau of Poyanne in France, subsequently entering a Jesuit house in

Portugal. With the Restoration, the Jesuits returned to Spain and Coloma was stationed at various houses, in La Guardia, Deusto, and finally Madrid, first at the boarding school in Chamartín de la Rosa and then at the house on Flor Baja street. During this long span of years he suffered from chronic ailments that caused him no little pain. In April 1891 he wrote the count of Guaqui: "Several things have prevented me from writing you, not the least of which has been the bad state of my liver, which has kept me in a continuous nausea." In December 1892 he wrote the duchess of Villahermosa that he was taking the new Brown-Lequand injections, which have cleared his head and shaken him from the depression that made "every serious occupation impossible for me." Apparently this depression became a constant in his life, for in April 1894 he wrote the same duchess: "On St. Joseph's day I was not, unfortunately, about to remember anything. On the vigil I suffered a headache that knocked me unconscious, and so I came to this College of Orduña to rest and recuperate. I am better now although I am always nervously excited, unusually so, which makes me understand perfectly what you are going through. Nothing can be compared to this general nervous depression, which produces a state very similar to madness."[16]

Like many writers of the nineteenth century, Luis Coloma had an ambivalent attitude toward his own era. Conscious that the customs of his day were superior to those of earlier centuries, he nevertheless found his heroes in St. Ferdinand III, Isabel the Catholic, and Cardinal Cisneros. He speaks of the "selfishness of our epoch" (see *OC*, 159, 189); he despises the newspapers, which he considers to be impious, devious, and disposed to untruth. A supporter of the original Restoration, he dislikes actual Restoration politics and its *barrer para adentro* (looking out for one's own interests), because, alas, the politicians did not restore Catholic unity to Spain: The Restoration is a Turkish warship with a Christian flag. And there are other elements one detects in his psychology upon reading his works over and over again; for example, his defensive reaction to such authors as Ernest Renan, the Frenchman who denied Christ's divinity and miracles, Joseph William Draper, the Anglo-American who professed to see a conflict between science and religion, and Miguel Mir, the Spaniard who left the Jesuit order and wrote a diatribe against it.[17] One other author of tremendous influence was Eugène Sue, whose *The Wandering Jew* (1844) excoriated the Jesuits. Coloma mentions Sue once, at the beginning of his story "¡¡Chist!!":

Well that house, friendly reader, that house is . . . . a house of Jesuits!!!!

Here the friendly reader's hair stands on end, he jumps up, and half frightened, half curious he goes over the facade of that mysterious house from the portal to the roof: he thinks he descries Father D'Aigrigny behind the door, Mademoiselle de Cardovelle at the window, the Indian Dejhar on the balcony, the Princess de Saint-Dizier at the rooftop, and his head peeping out the chimney, Rodin, the perfidious Rodin, who puts on his eyeglasses to see the one thing the friendly reader does not descry: the hundred bills of a thousand francs each that Mr. Eugène Sue pockets for the exhibition of these slanderous characters in the serial newspaper the *Constitutional,* a platform on which the revolutionary propaganda of 1848 set up its machinery for mowing down Jesuits.

Luis Coloma was on the defensive. He may have published an extremely provocative novel in 1891, *Bagatelles,* but the age was provocative and he felt he had good reason to do so.[18]

Coloma's Writings: The *Recreational Readings,* the Two Novels, and the Histories

Coloma's writings fall into three basic groups; his two score tales and stories entitled *Recreational Readings,* the two novels *Boy* and *Bagatelles,* and his historical studies, which lie between the genres of novel and biography. All his works, without exception, have a strong historical cast, originating in his view of history as a proof of moral teaching. For him the novelist is a missionary spreading the truth to receptive minds, and once the novelist preaches his particular truth, no matter what it might be, he can confidently turn to history for an exemplum. History will always support his argument: if he is preaching prudence and fortitude he will find examples of these virtues in the deeds of Queen Isabel and Cardinal Cisneros; piety?—he will find it in the devotion of a nineteenth-century *cesante,* an unemployed man put out of work by the Spanish political spoils system; resignation?—in the service and loyalty of Don John of Austria to his half-brother, Philip II; faith?—in the blind action of smugglers during the War of Independence, who return sacred vessels, stolen by the French, to the church.

In any account of Coloma's life, one of his works must be emphasized, *Bagatelles,* the long novel concerning King Amadeo's reign

(1870–73) and the Restoration Spain that followed. This novel produced one of the greatest sensations in Spanish literary history,[19] the issue being compounded by the special vocation of the author, a Jesuit priest. In one sense, Luis Coloma was unique, for in his uncompromising way he directed his primary satire at the traditional allies of the Jesuits, the aristocracy, rather than at the enemy, irreligious men, skeptics, and Freemasons. In the ensuing tumult, which contemporaries referred to as the *algarada* (shouting, din, the action of a band of marauders), he was attacked on all sides. According to one of the most recurrent criticisms, *Bagatelles* was a *novela de clave*, a novel of unnecessary individualization in which certain characters could be easily identified as persons in real life. In April 1891 the *Madrid Heraldo* opened its pages for two weeks so that anyone could send in a letter criticizing *Bagatelles.*[20]

The Royal Academy: The Final Years

Coloma was nominated for membership in the Royal Academy of Language on 2 January 1908, and submitted his entrance speech on 6 December of the same year. He was well received by his colleagues, there being only one vote cast against him.[21] In the Academy, Coloma chose as the subject of his address "The Author of *Fray Gerundio,*" Father José Francisco de Isla, a Jesuit priest and novelist of the eighteenth century. Coloma's vision of Isla, also a satirist, reveals a great deal of his own psychology. This long speech has recently been translated into English.[22]

Although the last decade of Coloma's life was marked by increasing ill health, he managed to publish during these years a series of biographies and the finished version of the novel his superiors had suppressed back in 1895. *The Marquis de Mora* appeared in 1903; *Jeromín,* the story of Don John of Austria, in 1903–7; the *Memories of Fernán Caballero* in 1907–10; *Boy* in 1910; and *Fray Francisco,* the story of Cardinal Cisneros, in 1911. For reasons of health, however, he removed himself from the world about him. He did not read his own Academy speech in 1908 but had the Marquis de Pidal read it for him, and from then until his death in 1915 he is known to have attended the Academy only once, in May 1909, when King Alfonso presided at a session creating the Fastenrath prize for literature. His life was one of constant suffering. He became deformed and was confined to a chair. He himself considered this to be an ascetic preparation for the life to come, a purgatory. His words to the duchess of Villahermosa will describe his inner life:

If you accept everything you suffer, physically or morally, with a profound resignation as coming from the hand of God, and if you offer everything to the Lord for the remission of your sins and the attainment of your desires, this *accepted mortification* will be able to equal and even surpass the voluntary penance you admire so much in those recluses; it can be equally pleasing in the eyes of God. . . . Each morning, offer to the Lord everything you are to suffer that day, as one sole act. . . .[23]

For Luis Coloma, the years of suffering were a prayer. The prayer ended 10 June 1915.

The fame of Luis Coloma diminished during his own lifetime, descending from the meteoric heights of the *Bagatelles* affair of 1891 to the unpublicized burial of a rather well-known author in 1915. During the last sixty years it has diminished even more, though not to the point of oblivion. His *Complete Works* have gone through four editions, the latest in 1960; *Bagatelles* has recently appeared in two editions (1968 and 1975);[24] *Boy* has been adapted to the stage and also made into a successful motion picture of the same title; films have been made of *Bagatelles* and *Jeromín*; and Coloma is studied every year by a small number of university students on both sides of the Atlantic. The critics in general have tended to ignore him, or disdain him if they find him too doctrinaire, but one of them, Rubén Benítez, has made a promising observation: "Coloma's novel requires a new focus, from the perspective of the experimental novel of the beginning of the twentieth century and not from that of the realist generation." With these words a new criticism has begun, and it is hoped that the present volume will contribute to it.

Chapter Two
Lecturas recreativas

Introduction

Luis Coloma wrote forty-one stories and tales for the religious magazine he helped to edit, the *Sacred Heart Messenger*. He later collected these pieces, gave them the general title of *Lecturas recreativas* (Recreational readings), and published them in five groups called *Scenes of Popular Customs, Miscellaneous Stories, Brush Strokes From Nature, New Brush Strokes*, and *Stories for Children*. These works, which were written for spiritual edification, have an emphatic, moralizing tone. The present chapter will examine several of them since they constitute almost a third of Coloma's writings.

The Aesthetics of Fernán Caballero

Coloma modeled his *Recreational Readings* on the literature of his elderly friend, Cecilia Böhl de Faber (Fernán Caballero), who explains her attitude toward art in chapter 7 of her novel, *La gaviota* (The seagull, 1849). Her explanation accurately describes the aesthetics of Luis Coloma. In *The Seagull* a young German doctor, Fritz Stein, comes to Andalusia and lives in an abandoned monastery with a Spanish family. On All Saints' Day, this family discusses religious customs and folklore, tells stories of a religious bent, and sings songs and lullabies referring to various plants and animals:

> There above, on Mount Calvary,
> little olive, fragrant bush,
> there sang the death of Christ
> four linnets and a nightingale.

The son Manuel introduces so many witty stories into the conversation that his mother must explain: "You can be sure, Don Federico, that there is no event for which my son doesn't have a story, joke, or witty anecdote, whether they come to the point or not." The boy is *pueblo*, the Spanish people, and after he comments on everything in his sententious way, the narrator, who is Fernán Caballero herself, enters the story to explain the nature of Spanish popular art, or *costumbrismo*:

It would be difficult for the person who catches these poetical emanations on the wing, as a boy catches butterflies, to explain to whoever might want to analyze them, why the nightingales and linnets lamented the death of the Redeemer; why the swallow pulled out the thorns from his crown; why the rosemary is looked on with a certain veneration, in the belief that the Virgin dried the diapers of the Child Jesus on a bush of that plant; why, or rather, how it is known that the elder tree is a sign of ill omen ever since Judas hung himself on one of them; why nothing bad ever happens in a house if incense from the rosemary is burned in it on Christmas night; why all the instruments of the Passion can be seen in the flower given that name. And, in truth, there are no answers for such questions. The people neither have answers nor seek them; they have gathered those things like the vague sound of a distant music, without inquiring into their origin or analyzing their authenticity. The *sages* and *positivists* will honor with a smile of disdainful compassion the person who writes these lines. But for us it is enough to hope to find some sympathy in the heart of a mother, or beneath the humble roof of him who knows little and feels much, or in the mystical retreat of a cloister, when we say that for our part we believe there have always been and there are today mysterious revelations for pious and ascetic souls. The world will call these revelations the delirium of overexcited imaginations, whereas the people of obedient and fervent faith will look upon them as special favors of God. Henri Blaze has said: "How many ideas tradition puts in the air in the form of a germ and the poet gives them life with his breath!" It seems to us that this very same thought applies to these things; it obliges no one to believe but also authorizes no one to condemn. A mysterious origin put the germ of them in the air, and believing and pious hearts give them life. No matter how much the apostles of rationalism prune the tree of faith, if the tree has its roots in good ground, that is, in a sound and fervent heart, it will eternally throw out vigorous and flowering branches that reach to heaven.

These thoughts of Fernán Caballero permeate the *Recreational Readings*. Coloma professes to be speaking for the people, specifically, the Andalusian people. There are poetical emanations in the air, like unfertilized germs, and the poet or storyteller breathes into them, giving them life. This picture resembles the doctrines of the Generation of 1898, Unamuno's intrahistory, for example, or Baroja's little things, Valle-Inclán's pantheistic gnosis, or Azorín's quotidian cock crowing, hammer sound on anvil, and locomotive glowing in the night—except for one thing: Luis Coloma's Spanish people (*pueblo*) are traditionalists. They believe in "God, King, and Country" and the "altar and the throne," so that the popular emanations will primarily contain the seeds of religion: a swallow easing the pain of the Crown of Thorns by removing one of them, nightingales and linnets lamenting the death of the divine redeemer, the rosemary as a drying place for the Infant Savior's garments. For Luis Coloma, like the boy Manuel in *The Seagull,* there is no event for which he does not have "a story, joke or witty anecdote" of a religious nature, "whether they are to the point or not." Perhaps the observations of the narrators in Coloma's stories relate to his theological point, but they frequently seem impertinent through overstatement, as in *Half John and John and a Half,* where the author himself enters at the end to explain why two Spanish smugglers return a shipment of gold chalices and ciboria, stolen by the French, to the Church. In a well-told story, the act of restitution alone will show the common man's deep devotion, and the narrative will require no final expository essay telling how all Spaniards, even smugglers and ne'er do wells, revere the Christian religion.[1] Now let us examine five stories.

"Un milagro"

"Un milagro" (A miracle), a story of some 4,200 words, is divided into five chapters, the first of which constitutes an apologia for the church's proclamation of miracles; and since the apologist is Coloma himself, the reader feels he has entered Coloma's chamber and caught him thinking out loud. He is irate, directing his anger at "a certain foreign academician,"[2] whom he quotes concerning miracles: "The modern thaumaturges have never shown me a resurrected dead man: the day they show me one, I shall believe in miracles." Needless to say, Coloma excoriates this position, and in this first, apologetic chapter he becomes carried away, employing every weapon at hand, italics, foreign words, sententious sayings, blunt statement, and sarcasm to buttress his religious argument. Since there is little attention to nuance, the reader may find that his confidence in the narrator has been shaken.[3]

The last four chapters of "A Miracle" call to mind the *Miracles of Our Lady,* by the thirteenth-century monk Gonzalo de Berceo. Felipe, a young man of good family, falls on evil ways because of his excessive ambition. He makes use of people to gain his selfish ends, and he has no saving graces whatsoever, but he carries in his pocket a Sacred Heart scapular that a gentlewoman mother superior had given him. One night at an opera, ashamed of the scapular, he hides it and loses it, only to find that an American lady gives him one just like it the next day. He repents and leads an exemplary life until his death two years later, thus fulfilling the promise of Jesus to St. Margaret Mary: "I will bless the places where they keep the image of my Heart."

At the end, Coloma the narrator enters the story again to answer the "certain foreign academician's" remark about modern thaumaturges: "And is this the resurrection of a dead man? Yes! It is the resurrection of a dead soul, a miracle more stupendous than returning a cadaver to life; for whereas the latter requires all the power of God, the former requires in addition to all his power, all his mercy." Coloma's logic and storytelling may be found wanting here, but were he completely logical and artistic he would not be Luis Coloma, the passionate man who saw his most cherished beliefs under attack. He must pick up the challenge. And he did, with stories such as "A Miracle."

¿"Qué sería?"

¿Qué sería?" (What could it be) divagates as the narrator attempts to gain the reader's confidence. The year is 18** and the protagonist Adela de M**, the asterisks purporting to create an air of insouciance between the narrator and the friendly, discreet reader ("Friendly reader!" . . . "Here I must confess to you, discreet reader. . . . ") This insouciance is belied by the narrator's talk of Moltke, Bismarck, Napoleon III, the Ems Affair, the battle of Sedan, Kaiser Wilhelm, and by his association of the mysterious Adela de M** with the notorious Georges Sand.

After the long, circuitous introduction, a septuagenarian lady visits the narrator seeking spiritual advice, for he is a Jesuit priest; she is none other than Adela de M**, the mysterious woman who lived in France with two nocturnal women, Georges Sand and Delfina Gay. Although she was like them an unbeliever, her woman's honor has never been questioned. When she returned to Spain to "bury herself in the ancient home of her elders," people nicknamed her Rabina (Rabina, or Rabbi, suggests Faustian powers). At this point the narrator mentions two authors whose names are a clue not only to the nature of this story but to the nature of many of the *Recreational Readings*: Hoffman and Klopstock. He speaks of "that fantastic character of Hoffman, which had lost its shadow, turning its head every moment to see if the shadow was still following it"; and then he alludes to the Rabina's old companion, a domestic devil—"if it was in fact a domestic devil, it must have been a contrite devil, like the Abdiel-Abbadona Klopstock dreamed up." Here is the key to this story, E. T. A. Hoffman and Friedrich Gottlieb Klopstock; Hoffman, the creator of literary phantasmagoria, and Klopstock, the creator of religious poetry. Coloma is writing a fantastic story *a lo divino,* as Spaniards say, that is, he has taken the stories of writers like Hoffman and adapted them to his religious message.[4] *A lo divino* stories end well, for their theme is redemption. At the end of "What Could It Be?" an apparition of her sister appears to Adela de M**, who then carries out the dead woman's will. She herself, the former confidante of French atheists, dies well shriven and in the odor of sanctity.

One line of "What Could It Be?" contains the language of the medieval school. Adela de M** (The Rabina) questions the narrator about the apparition: "This is what frightens me. . . . Do you think it's possible that the soul of a dead person come from the other world to stop others from ceasing to pray for her?" The narrator answers: "Yes, Madam, I replied firmly. I believe it's possible, but in my judgment not probable. I believe it's possible because everything comes under the power of God, and if you will concede to me that God exists, you cannot deny me his attributes, and if you do not deny me his attributes, neither can you deny me that he may exercise them." Although Coloma was trained in the Scholastic tradition, he rarely writes in this antiquated philosophical style.[5]

Two Historical Stories: "Las borlitas de Mina" and "La batalla de los cueros"

Coloma made a point of staying close to history, which was, as he saw it, a storehouse of examples for the lessons he was teaching. Two stories showing his proximity to history are "Las borlitas de Mina" (The tassels of Mina) and "La batalla de los cueros" (The battle of the hides), but they differ from his other stories since in them he curbs his didactic impulses. Francisco Javier Mina (1789–1817), the guerrilla leader from Navarre, became an implacable enemy of the French after they pillaged his native town Idocín, leaving his parents impoverished. He won so many victories that the Spanish governor of Lérida supplied arms for his men and the central Junta honored him by assigning him his own flag. Mina's determination and bravery were never questioned, by friend or foe. "The Tassels of Mina" begins: "In February of 1811 Marshall Suchet put a price on the heads of Mina and his two lieuten-

ants. Six thousand *duros* he offered for the head of the chief *guerrillero,*
four thousand for that of the second in command, Don Gregorio Cru-
chaga, and two thousand for that of Gorriz or anyone else who was his
equal." The narrator resorts to the *cancionero* (the popular songs of
Spain), advising the reader that as a boy Mina learned the following
stanza:

> San Luis, rey de Francia, es
> el que con Dios pudo tanto
> que para que fuese santo
> le dispensó el ser francés.
> St. Louis, king of France,
> God knew was very good,
> so to crown his saintly hood
> He forgave his French nuance.[6]

Mina took this and other similar stanzas so much to heart that his sole
ambition in life became the killing of Napoleon's soldiers.

In one foray Mina's brave highlanders capture a shipment of French
uniforms consisting of red trousers and short blue jackets with red
tassels in front and rear. The highlanders refuse to don the uniforms
though ordered to do so and Mina is about to decimate them for want
of discipline, when a little bugle boy explains: "The tassels? . . .
Whooo! . . . They're for sissies." Mina finally relents but threatens to
place his men always in the vanguard, to which they reply: "The vanguard yes! . . . The tassels no!"

"The Battle of the Hides" took place in 1325 when the city of Jerez
was attacked by a large host of Moors. The *jerezanos* were on the verge
of despair until the great knight Cosme Damián D'Avila conceived the
ruse of tying brambles, thorns, and crude leather hides to the tails of
the ponies. Then the Christians created a tumult (*algazara*), the ponies
charged, and in the ensuing confusion the Moorish host was frightened
and dispersed. This story and "The Tassels of Mina" resemble the "national stories" ("historietas nacionales") of Pedro Antonio de Alarcón
(1833–91). Their value is in the historical anecdote.

Coloma's "Feigned Narration": "El primer baile"

According to Coloma, "El primer baile" (The first ball) differs from
all his other stories because it is nonhistorical. In a prologue composed
for the *Recreational Readings* he wrote:

It is in this sense and only and exclusively in this sense that the editors of the *Sacred Heart Messenger* publish this modest little volume of tales, novelistic certainly in their form, but all of them based on historical facts, which make them differ essentially from the novel, whose plot always starts out from fantasy. Only one of these *Tales,* "The First Ball," is a feigned narration from a thousand true episodes: it is a voice of warning to innocence and a shout of reproach to malice, since the former is in danger of succumbing and the latter about to triumph at certain types of dances which, although we do not believe they are *always* sinful, we believe that sometimes through prudence and other times through necessity they should *always* be avoided, because they are in a greater or lesser degree dangerous. No moralist has expressed the unsuitability of these dances as forcefully perhaps as Goethe, the immoral poet, the singer of suicidal *heroes* and impure loves, over whom devout fears and social respect held so little sway. In his famous book *Werther,* Werther writes to William, after having waltzed with Charlotte: "I will tell you frankly, William, I then swore to myself that the woman I loved and over whom I had some authority would never waltz with anyone but me; never, although it cost me my life. Do you understand?"

May the readers of the *Messenger* accept the dedication of these *Recreational Readings* as a weapon that the love of the divine heart places in their hands to attract gently to good literature all those souls whose frivolity, whose lukewarmness, or whose prejudices impede them from seeking in more serious literature the teachings and ways of love of Jesus Christ. Saint Basil says that "the first step for raising oneself to perfection is to remove oneself from evil; in the same way that the first step for ascending a staircase is to raise one's foot from the ground."

May these *Recreational Readings* then be the first step that will remove souls from bad novels, those many souls that can and should find solace and profit in works like *The Guide for Sinners* and the *Imitation of Christ.* (*OC,* 61)

Two things are to be considered in the above passage, and they should not be confused, the morality of Coloma and his literary theory. As a moralist he points to three guides, St. Basil (the fourth century), Friar Luis de Granada (*The Guide for Sinners,* sixteenth century), and Thomas à Kempis (*Imitation of Christ,* fifteenth century). Following Basil and Luis de Granada he presents the doctrine of the proximate and remote occasions of sin, the former of which must always be avoided. From his experience in aristocratic circles and presumably the confessional he argues that certain kinds of dances are *always* proximate occasions, even when they appear not to be. Following Kempis he argues for detachment from the things of this world, which would include of course dances, even good dances, a doctrine not immensely appealing, one should think, to the debutantes of 1884. As for the judgments concerning Goethe and "bad novels," presumably French novels, Coloma the moralist has entered the controversial area where literature and morality meet. Cervantes's invective against the books of chivalry and Mariano José de Larra's objection to the sentimental novels read by young women reveal judgments similar to his, although they are never so austere.[7]

The literary theory of the passage cited above is less easily defined. Coloma says that "The First Ball" is the only "feigned narration" of his *Recreational Readings,* which calls to mind the theory of earlier centuries, when imaginative literature was called a lie. It is the only feigned narration, that is to say, the only lie, the only fiction. It is not historical, it is a figment, he alone has made it up, but even so it is based on "a thousand true episodes," the sum of his experience. In other words, Luis Coloma would have his readers believe that all his stories except one, no matter how cloying or farfetched the reader may find them, are rather like chronicles or newspaper articles repeating facts of their author's experience; whereas "The First Ball" is a composite based on a "thousand true episodes" and is characteristically true although its details have been invented. Thus all the stories but one have truth, and the one has verisimilitude.

It would appear that Coloma was so convinced of certain subjective truths that they became objective and scientific for him. Thus he can say that a spiritual event like the salvation of a sinful soul (see the story "A Miracle") is a miracle, whereas miracles should be something palpable; they should be events of this world that the eye (not the inner eye) can see, the hand touch, or the ear hear. And having said it is a miracle, he acts as if this miracle and miracles in general were scientifically true, just as it is true that two parts of hydrogen and one part of oxygen are the components of water. Why? Because he believes it. By casually confusing experience and belief, the seen and the unseen, the quotidian and the miraculous, the commonplace and the mysterious, in a word, the natural and the supernatural, Coloma seems to do the latter a disfavor. By diminishing the supernatural, he is apt to make it look ridiculous.

"The First Ball" is the most didactic of the *Recreational Readings.* A marchioness is anxious to have her daughter Lulú attend a ball so that she can meet a certain young duke and lure him into matrimony. The girl is reluctant to go because the décolleté fashions of the day strike her as indecent. Her uncle supports her arguments, which infuriates the marchioness, and a debate follows. Finally, the two women attend the festivities. Upon her return Lulú has a dream and then dies. It is here that "The First Ball" differs from the other stories, for Coloma, having posed his doctrine of modesty and that of scandal, looks not to history for his example but to the world of dreams.

In Lulú's dream she is waltzing and the young duke squeezes his hand into her side, causing her pain. Suddenly there is no light or floor beneath her feet, but a wet sticky soil giving chills, and a music of fipple flutes and owls rather than violins. The duke's hand is like a claw in her side now, causing her atrocious pain and from his handsome person there comes a filthy brilliance that does not touch her but that she herself, not knowing how, has lit. His eyes are fixed on her face and neck like two poisonous darts, and nevertheless she keeps waltzing and waltzing at her mother's command. There is nobody there to help her. Then:

Suddenly she saw in the distance, without knowing how, a group of trees, and a man prostrate on the earth, as they portray Jesus in the garden of olives. Lulú shouted: Dear Jesus! and Jesus arose at that cry, handsome, strong, forceful, with his wounded Heart in his hands, as she had seen him so often on the altar at school, as she had just seen him in the icon at the prie-dieu, but the duke kept waltzing without releasing his prey, and he roared at times fiercely. Jesus raised his hand with authority and ordered him to stop: but the duke raised his own without releasing Lulú and slapped the cheek of Christ.

Pardon me, my Jesus, for I am the cause! shouted Lulú, wringing her hands.

Jesus took two steps back and threw a handful of his own blood on the ground to stop the duke; but the duke didn't let Lulú go and kept waltzing over the blood of Christ.

Pardon, Jesus mine, for I am to blame—moaned Lulú, pulling her hair.

And Jesus, to save the girl, threw on the ground, at the duke's feet, his heart swollen with anguish.

But the duke kept waltzing without letting Lulú go, and he raised his foot to step on Christ's Heart.

Lulú gave a frightful cry and found herself awake seated on her bed. There on an arm chair was the white dress for the ball; there on the prie-dieu, the image of Christ: in her right side the poor girl felt the horrible pain the iron hand of the duke caused in her dreams. The sunlight was coming into the bedroom through the rose-colored curtains, giving everything a cheerful hue.

At Lulú's shout her maid came running; after her, the anxious marchioness. Lulú, pale, her face distorted, her eyes bulging out of their sockets, coughing in a way that froze the blood, stretched forth her arms to her mother, who, weeping, embraced her:

Mama, mama, said Lulú in such a quiet, deep voice that it was terrifying

to hear her: There! . . . There! . . . at the ball . . . in the garden . . . the
duke stepped on blood. . . . I didn't. . . . I didn't sin! . . . no, no, my
God! . . . but through my fault . . . through my fault that man stepped on
Christ's blood!
And a terrible convulsion twisted the body of the unhappy girl, like the
rings of a snake.

In this sulphurous passage the theme of scandal, the leading of another
person into sin, typifies the thought of Luis Coloma; one will find it
in his other stories, in his novels, and in his novelistic biographies,
such as *The Marquis de Mora*. The dream, however, with its phallic
symbolism and erotic dance, is unusual.

The *Recreational Readings*: Conclusion

In the *Recreational Readings* Luis Coloma attempts to instruct and
entertain his readers through historical and feigned narration. An example of Coloma's historical narration is "A Miracle," in which a scapular effects the conversion of a young sinner; an example of his feigned
narration is "The First Ball," where a young girl's whirlwind dream
dance teaches the meaning of sexual scandal. The distinction between
the two narrations is perhaps less clear to the reader than it was to their
author, who in "A Miracle" engages in extrahistorical intervention with
his placement of the second scapular, his belief in the divine words
spoken to St. Margaret Mary, and his equalizing the figurative resurrection of a dead soul with a miracle raising a dead man to life. In
stories like "A Miracle" Coloma did not sufficiently distinguish between religious faith, rational probability, and the incontrovertible
data of history. It may also be that he unwittingly gave occasion to
unbelievers to laugh, by urging noncogent arguments and examples as
demonstrations of faith.[8]
In "The First Ball" the reader might argue that although the dance
and erotic frenzy are well executed, the narrator tends to divide his
reading audience into those who agree with his moral teaching and
those who do not; thus some readers will feel isolated, whereas a work
of art should be unitive. Be that as it may, in the year 1891, when
Father Luis Coloma was forty years of age, he brought his historical
and feigned narration together in his most famous book, *Bagatelles*.

Chapter Three
Pequeñeces

Pequeñeces (Bagatelles)[1] consists of four books and an epilogue that are only slightly asymmetrical: they have, respectively, 11, 8, 8, 9, and 1 chapters. Since Book 1, chapter 1, is in effect a prologue setting the tone of the novel and since the epilogue returns to the theme of chapter 1, the balance is almost perfect. In the Jesuit school of chapter 1, which is "an oasis of copses of lilies" and where "the water gushes in the fountains and runs along the troughs murmuring," the young boys are happy. The outside world makes some impression there, but in this oasis the boys are protected from spiritual thirst. The narrator asks: "Oh sorrowful Virgin of Recollection, will they remember you?" Some of the boys will not remember, just as their parents do not in books 1–4, but it is always possible this side of death to return to the oasis.

In the epilogue, the oasis theme reappears when the wanton sinner, Countess Currita de Albornoz, comes to the Sanctuary of Loyola. Because of her misconduct she has lost her son in the fierce waters of an undertow, but now she has come to the oasis to hear Mass. One of her victims is there, the Marchioness of Sabadell, whose son also drowned because of Currita's misconduct and whose heart has dried up: she could not "wring out one lone tear, as if the spring of tears were already dried up in her heart. . . ." But the saving waters are there, for after the Mass the Marchioness cries, and going up to Currita "she placed her hand in the holy water font and offered it to her with the tip of her fingers. . . ." The school of chapter 1 and Sanctuary of the epilogue are the Augustinian City of God with the saving waters of grace, and between them in the four books we see the Earthly City where the waters are fetid pools (*hediondas charcas*), mud slush (*fango*), and *ciénagas* (swamps), or oceanic undertows drowning innocent victims.

Chapter 1 may also be considered from another vantage point: the school with its innocent youth is the Garden of Eden, where the serpent has not yet made his appearance; but he will soon come, for the school is an island in a sterile desert, and on the horizon not so far away lies Madrid, the court of Spain, "una hedionda charca" (fetid pool). The Serpent will come through Madrid's bad example, which will be seen on many occasions in books 1–4. In chapter 1, the intruding narrator makes his presence felt in various ways. Where children are concerned, he employs an excessively affectionate diminutive. A child has little eyes, a little voice, little hands, a little head, a little breast, a little face, little teeth, little brothers, and if he attends a graduation alone, without his parents, he is a poor little fellow. The narrator is a sentimental person who never hesitates to favor or disfavor his characters; later on he will resort to his store of derogatory expressions, his augmentatives so to speak, to describe libertines and Freemasons whom he associates with the Earthly City and even with the Serpent.

Explicitly or implicitly, chapter 1 reveals everything in the narrator's argument. A thesis is not mentioned as such, but the narrator is clearly not just an Augustinian Christian, but also a philo-aristocrat:

A child white and fair, beautiful and candorous like an angel of Fray Angelico, came forward then to the middle of the dais: the charm of his age and innocence was heightened by that aristocratic and delicately fine *ese no sé qué* which in the children of great houses attracts, subjugates, and is even touching; and his long reddish head of hair, cut in front like that of a fifteenth-century page, gave him the look of that prince Richard whom Millais painted in his famous picture *The Sons of Edward*.

What the narrator omits here is perhaps even more important than what he says. Since the sons of Edward were all murdered by their uncle, a member of their own family, it follows that the noble youth of the school (the oasis, the Garden of Eden), noble by their innocence and social class, may also be murdered if only figuratively when they enter the fetid pool of Madrid. Chapter 2 will make an abrupt transition to the fetid pool, too abrupt for the critics of the nineteenth century who felt that the novel should have begun with chapter 2. But in the narrator's eyes they must have been wrong, for how can one understand the muddy waters if he has not first seen the oasis with its refreshing vegetation?

The first chapter also contains sixty verses recited to the Virgin of Recollection on graduation day, stanzas of which prefigure the books of the novel. One stanza reads:

> They say the world's a pleasant garden
> with asps occult therein . . .
> that sweet fruit has fatal venom,
> that the sea of the world is filled with reefs . . .
> and why must it be so?

These prosaic verses not only contain the Augustinian City of God–City of Earth theme; line 4 (the sea of the world) forebodes the drowning in book 4, chapter 9 of Alfonsito and Paco. Another stanza reads:

> They say that for gold and honor
> faithless men of vile heart
> dry up the fount of their love
> betraying both God and country . . .
> why must it be so?

In these verses the narrator has entered the political arena, since the line "y a su Dios y a su patria son traidores" (betraying both God and country) refers to the Glorious Revolution of 1868, which changed the constitution of Spain. Revolutionaries are men of evil, Freemasons, who undermine the two supports of civilized society, God and the throne.

Chapter 1 attempts to create the novelistic equivalent of a sonnet. Clinging to the original idea of the heavenly and earthly cities, it ends with the refrain: "Oh sorrowful Virgin of Recollection, / will they remember you?" Those who remember the Virgin and the heavenly oasis she reigned over when they were young will eventually find their way home, and those who do not will condemn themselves to outer darkness. That is what *Bagatelles* is all about.

The change is abrupt in chapter 2. Whereas the first chapter is idyllic with a narrator patently using diminutives and making traditionalist judgments, the intruding narrator has now disappeared, or almost disappeared, for he declares that the wealthy Mrs. López Moreno "is as fat as her husband's money bags." The reader finds himself in the world of the realistic novel of the 1880s and 1890s. The hirsute Marquis of Butrón, some fops and the *alfonsinas,* the ladies opposing King Amadeo I, are gathered in the *fumoir* of the Duchess of Bara. The women are smoking cigars and sipping whisky, an affectation of the period, and the conversation is studded with French words, *matinée, brioches, pendant,* "O mon Dieu; quel gros mot!," and others. As the ladies discuss their Restoration politics, their snideness converges on the absent Currita Albornoz, whose family are grandees of Spain. At the chapter's end Currita enters: "Through the door of the *fumoir* they all saw come forth, from the neighboring room, a very tiny thin lady who walked with little steps on her high heels, tapping the floor with the tip of the long handle of her lace parasol. She had red hair, a face full of freckles, and her gray pupils were so clear they seemed to expunge themselves at a distance, giving the strange effect of the dead eyes of a statue." Coloma's critics have frequently singled out chapter 2 as the best passage of *Bagatelles* and have usually preferred Currita Albornoz to his other characters, even wryly remarking that his sinful creations are superior to his virtuous ones. Perhaps there is an aesthetic truth here; perhaps, owing to man's fragile nature, it is easier to portray wayward people than those who keep to the road.

Book 1, Chapter 3

Since Coloma was writing in chapter 2 what the critics of his day desired, a realistic novel, they could accept it. In chapter 3, however, the satire begins with its attendant exaggeration, and from here on the characters, institutions, and ideas are fair game. Many of the Madrid residents of Coloma's day could no more accept the satire and attitudes of *Bagatelles* than the birth control advocate Margaret Sanger could accept Evelyn Waugh's *Black Mischief* or a sensitive African enjoy Pío Baroja's European tribal satire *Paradox, King.* Chapter 3 can speak for itself:

The twenty-first of June, 1832, Ferdinand VII, dragging his feet because of his gout and years, and María Cristina, at the very height of her charm and beauty, were taking from the baptismal font in the collegial and parochial Church of the Most Holy Trinity, of the Royal Palace of San Ildefonso, a child called Ferdinand, Christian, Robustianus, Charles, Louis Gonzaga, Alphonse of the Most Holy Trinity, Anacletus, Vincent.

He was the primogeniture son of the Marquis and Marchioness of Villamelón, grandees of Spain, he a gentleman consort of His Majesty the King, and a maid of honor she of Her Majesty the Queen. He was the last child that Ferdinand godfathered in this vale of tears; fifteen months later the latter descended to his sepulchre in the Royal Palace of Madrid, fulfilling to the letter the simile of the bottle of beer to which the sly monarch used to compare his people. He was the cork that was popping out, the revolution the foamy liquid that was spreading on all sides. That very afternoon Ferdinand wanted to examine his godson closely, and in his own living room, plunged in his armchair, he put the newborn child on his knees, opened his little mouth with a finger, and placed his nose of pure Bourbon race inside, as if he wanted to examine the opening of his esophagus. The case was portentous, and Ferdinand, frightened on verifying it, removed his nose promptly. . . . The tender Villamelón had come into the world with a complete set of teeth. Henry IV was born with two teeth, Mirabeau with two molars, and he who surpassed in such a way the great king and outdid the famous tribune, necessarily must also be the source of great things.

Villamelón the father was weeping with joy, and the Count of Alcudia, present at the time, advised him that he use for the nursing of his son the twenty-seven cows and forty she-goats then serving as wetnurses for the baby hippopotamus, the gift of Abbas-Pacha, which was being raised in Paris, in the Botanical Gardens. But Ferdinand opined that they let him suck on chops, and that they wean him later on brandy, and that very night he sent his godson, as a present from his godfather, a great carving knife of solid gold, with the arms of Spain sculpted on the handle.

The queen also wanted to verify the prodigy by putting the tip of her pink finger in the mouth of little Villamelón, and Don Thaddeus Calomarde, who arrived at that moment, wanted to try the same experiment, introducing his own finger, stained with ink. But the child then forcefully squeezed his precocious pincers causing the minister to let out a light shriek.

You can see he's not a fool—said Ferdinand VII.

Chapter 3 begins with the birth of a modern "hero," and so the date must be precise: it is the twenty-first of June, 1832, the first day of summer, an augury of prodigious growth. A baptism is taking place and the sponsor is no less than Ferdinand VII, the Bourbon king of Spain; and the place a Royal Palace named for San Ildefonso; and the child a baby whose many baptimal names evoke sanctity, Spain, all of Christendom, the Holy Roman Empire, and even God the Father, Son, and Holy Ghost. He is a grandee of Spain, a *mayorazgo,* and . . . and then there is mention of gout and beer, of old age and suds. This juxtaposition of matter and spirit calls to mind the funeral address described by Henri Bergson in his book on the causes of laughter: "The deceased was noble and fat." The name Villamelón is also significant, for although it begins well it ends with *melón,* a melon or fool. The baby Villameloncito is a little fool.

The narrator of chapter 3 reserves his special barbs for Spanish liberals. A foolish grandee may be the object satirized here, but the satire is directed at liberals of any class. To mention the name of Ferdinand

VII is gall, and the beer-cork metaphor is the essence of gall. Liberal
historians referred to the reign of Ferdinand (1823–33) as the Ominous
Decade and Ferdinand himself was "the worst man who ever lived."
The foaming revolution pouring out of a bottle does not suggest so
much the French Revolution and European Revolutions of 1830 and
1848 as the Spanish Glorious Revolution of 1868 and its aftermath,
the Restoration, not the ideal restoration the young Luis Coloma had
envisioned but a compromising revolution that did not return the altar
and throne to their former position. If Ferdinand is called the sly monarch (*socarrón monarca*) then the narrator must also be called *socarrón*,
sly, that is to say, a satirist. He can censure or ridicule whomever and
whatever he wants, providing he is not culpable of overstatement. And
here perhaps is the flaw in book 1, chapter 3 of *Bagatelles*, and in the
entire novel: in paragraph 8 the narrator makes a statement that had
better been left unsaid. Paragraphs 1 to 6 have already been translated;
here are 7 and 8:

Everyone laughed at the wit of the monarch, and the phrase left the royal
living room, went across the other rooms, passed through the anterooms, and
as it went down the stairways everyone was already commenting on it. People,
amazed at the talent of the baby, were asserting that three days after its birth
it was reciting to its august godfather the Our Father, Hail Mary, part of the
Loreto Litany, and a little fable of Don Thomas Iriarte, the one that begins:

> In among the bushes
> with many dogs at heel,
> I will not say there ran,
> there was flying a rabbit. . . .

The case was prodigious, and one dated the fame of the man of talent, who
was to be the future Marquis of Villamelón, from that time on, until the
repeated vigor of his stupidities ruined the whole thing.

The adult Villamelón is a coward, a fool, a glutton, an ass, a slothful
man, an aristocratic *cabrón* (cuckold) who consents to the infidelity of
his own wife. He is the scorn of Madrid's high society and by the
novel's end has become an old, doddering idiot accompanying his wife
everywhere, more like an ambulatory vegetable than a dog. His deformation is so great that there is no need of a clause like "until the
repeated vigor of his stupidities ruined the whole thing," a pleonasm

tarnishing the satire and suggesting that behind the narrator there lurks another being with a string in his hand pulling the marionettes a bit too much in order to vent his spleen. This other being of course is Coloma himself, the novelist-missionary who overstated his case so frequently in the *Recreational Readings*. Nevertheless, his intervention is less frequent in *Bagatelles* and the tarnish not so universal.

The rest of chapter 3 develops the character of Villamelón and his wife, "an illustrious savage completely naked of soul," Doña Francisca de Borja Solís y Gorbea, Countess of Albornoz, Marchioness of Catañalzor, whose lengthy titles rival those of her august spouse. In depicting Villamelón, the narrator invokes the art of Francisco de Quevedo, in whose picaresque novel *The Swindler* Pablos witnesses a naval battle, or *nabal* battle ("batalla nabal"), *nabal* sounding like *naval* in Spanish but meaning *turnip* ("a turnip battle"). Similarly, Villamelón's putative exploits at the Battle of Cabo Negro in 1859, where he fled from the "ill-mannered Rifs," are converted by a witticism of Queen Isabel from deeds at the "*terro-naval* combat of Cabo Negro" to the "*navo-terrestre*" combat. Villamelón, so to speak, is a turnip.

The narrator's portrait of Villamelón's wife, through her actions and her words, is a memorable part of the novel. In her vanity she must outdo everyone in order to attract attention. Unlike the other women she smokes a stogie that would fell a sergeant, rather than a cigar; she is proud of her husband's mailing a letter with King Amadeo's head on the stamp upside down; she humiliates another countess; she pretends to be secretive when there is no call for secrecy; she puns at a political demonstration where a hunchback carries a flag calling for reform; she has her beet-faced English coachman drive her carriage pell-mell through a crowd; she embarrasses King Amadeo's wife by pretending to want the post of first lady-in-waiting; and she postpones seeing her young son who has just returned from boarding school (the unfortunate child of chapter 1).

There is still some intrusion from beyond the frame of the novel. A parenthetical clause reads: "And although no one perhaps could have explained the reason for this supremacy that Currita enjoyed at court, nevertheless, with that shameful accomodation of the scandalous, which is in our judgment the capital sin of high society in Madrid and the origin and source of all its deformities, everybody. . . ." *Our judgment*: Luis Coloma the missionary has entered the novel without a by-your-leave. He does so again six pages later by using a subjunctive of conjecture, the conjecturer being himself: "*Barrer para adentro* was

Butrón's politics, as if garbage could serve anywhere for anything other than infesting the area around it." The marvel of *Bagatelles* is its ability to survive these intrusions. It is, despite them, a fine novel capturing the mood of the aristocracy during Restoration Spain.

Book 1, Chapters 4–9

Chapters 4–9 picture the life of high society in Madrid with its basic ennui. Everything must be done by the socialites to catch the attention of others, to create a sensation. When the young school boy of chapter 1 returns home, he is received not by his parents, Currita and Villamelón, but by the family dwarf Don Joselito and the other seventeen servants. In the vestibule of his house stands a huge stuffed Norwegian bear with a card tray in his paws, and in Currita's room, the statue of a life-size nude Negro, carved in ebony, sustaining a lamp. Scandal is desirable provided it attracts attention, for scandalous conduct gone unnoticed is a *pifia* (blunder). A rather unusual event, the search of Currita's palace by the police, is reported in the newspapers as a precursor of the guillotine, another 1793! The ladies at the opera are apt to wear two-colored outfits and two different colored gloves to match. A fatal duel provides the opportunity for egolatrous advertisement (chapter 11).

The demonstration of mantillas and *peinetas* (a large Spanish comb worn in the hair) against Amadeo's government provides the ladies a chance to be seen on the boulevard. Gossip is the order of the day, especially when a high figure is brought low; the morning of the police search an agitated Marquis of Butrón forgot to dye his beard and was seen in public with black hair and white beard, which was followed by a newspaper comment: "They tell the story of Charles V, that on visiting a monastery in Germany one day he saw a monk who had a black beard and completely white hair. He asked him the cause of this strange phenomenon, and the monk replied:—Sire, I have worked more with my head than my teeth." With the Marquis of Butrón it is the other way around, black hair and white beard.

One clause of chapter 10 reveals the art of the preceding chapters: the narrator refers to "the great social punchinello (*polichinela*), dressed up in all human misery and ridiculousness." Punchinello, the buffoon or clown of the Italian *commedia dell'arte,* provides the key to the art of *Bagatelles,* whose characters are frequently the *fantoches* or marionettes of a satire. They should not be judged exclusively by the norms of the realist novel, where author-puppeteers are unwelcome, but by the norms of satirical art where characters are deformed and frequently moved by strings. Thus in *Bagatelles* there are perhaps three critical positions to be taken.

First, the narrator tells a story independent of the missionary-novelist envisioned by Father Luis Coloma, S. J., in his prologue. This independent narrator can be frequently observed in *Bagatelles*; for example, in the letter-burning scene of book 1, chapter 5, where Currita orders a huge fire to be built in her fireplace, on a hot 25 June! She has complained of a headache to the minister of the interior, Don Juan Antonio Martínez, *el buey Apis,* and he replies:

"Why don't you put two slices of potatoes on your temples? That's very comforting."

"Potatoes?," exclaimed Currita, shuddering in consternation. "Good God, Martínez, I prefer the headache."

Martínez realized that his country bumpkin ways were sticking out from under the minister's skin, and he set about his business, leaving aside compassive prologues and home recipes.

"I am sorry then to add to your headache, but the business is grave and urgent. . . ."

Martínez has a compromising letter, written by Currita's husband, that she is anxious to destroy, and so when he reads it to her by the fireside she listens carefully and:

suddenly, with the agility of a predatory cat springing on an unwary mouse, she snatched the dangerous letter from the minister's hands and threw it into the fire. . . . The paper curled up for a moment in the flames, and then became ashes.

The astonished minister drew back quickly in his armchair, letting out an obscenity; but Currita, not being offended by it, nor surprised either, eased herself back on her pillow as though nothing had happened, saying with her candid little laugh: "Come, come, Martínez! . . . You'll have to put on two potato plasters. . . . They're very soothing!"

There are many passages like this in *Bagatelles,* and they require no apology.

The second critical position concerns the narrator's role as a puppeteer making fun of dandies, fops, hypocrites, social climbers, backbiters, and other insidious people. Although there is some danger of

Coloma the missionary's appearing here, the narrator without his help
frequently achieves satirical deformation bordering on puppetry. An
example of this appears in book 1, chapter 9, where Villamelón comes
upon twenty-five love letters to his wife from an artillery captain. In
the third letter he encounters the phrase *cucurbitácea*: "As for your husband, let us just suppress the *villa* for him and keep the *melón*; it has
been proved that the poor man belongs to the family of the *cucurbitá-
ceas.*" Villamelón the cuckold grandee of Spain, is now a *villamelón*
minus *villa,* that is to say, a *melón,* a dolt or idiot. Instead of trying to
avenge his dishonor or to stop the artillery captain's successor, Juanito
Velarde, from making love to his wife, he goes about looking for the
meaning of *cucurbitácea.* What can it be? Everyone he asks either shrugs
his shoulders or laughs, until he comes to the crapulous gentleman
whose cynical ways have earned him the nickname of Diogenes:

His name was Pedro de Viva, he was the second born of a great house, he
lived from gambling when he wasn't drunk, and his cynicism and dirty stories
had made him famous in Madrid. Everyone knew him by the name of Diogenes. He was one of those persons who have come to be known for certain
things, and once in possession of that executorship they can freely commit all
sorts of excesses with no other fear than of seeing people shrugging their
shoulders and murmuring: That's his way!

Villamelón, or rather the punchinello, Melón, the fool, asks Diogenes:

"Diogenes! . . . You who know everybody, can you tell me what the family
of *cucurbitácea* is? . . ."
Diogenes stared at him for a moment, undoubtedly thinking that one
knows the foolishness or wisdom of a man more quickly through his questions
than his answers, and at last he said to him: "I should say so! Come here!" . . .
And taking him up to a mirror, and grabbing him by the nape of the neck,
with the other hand he gave him a loud slap on the head, saying very seriously:
"Here you have the mother. . . ." Then he shouted insolently in his ear:

> Let him not brag he's somethin'
> he who should be a melon and's a pumpkin.

Like a figure from the *commedia dell'arte* this buffoon is a pumpkin, a
dimwit. The missionary-novelist may appear before or after scenes like
this, but he does not enter them.
The third critical position concerns the appearance of the mission-

ary-novelist, intruding on the domain of the story he has written. Luis Coloma does this in various ways. Sometimes in a footnote he merely translates foreign words he has used: "In England the special apartment where the children live isolated from the rest of the family is called the *Nursery*" (chapter 4); "What's that, Miss? You have to learn your piano lesson until eight o'clock." "¿Qué es eso, Miss? Hay que estudiar la lección de piano hasta las ocho" (chapter 4). Or he will write a short footnote saying "Histórico todo" ("This is all historical": a reference to the episode in which a pimp and a couple of prostitutes break up the demonstration of mantillas and *peinetas*). These interventions may seem simple enough, but they evoke the presence of the Luis Coloma of *Recreational Readings,* who wanted to prove everything and to show that everything was historical in order to gain the credence of the reader. Perhaps footnotes of this kind were better written by editors than authors, that is to say, perhaps authors should not edit.

In *Bagatelles* some sentences and paragraphs pass judgments on the characters not in keeping with the detached style of other passages. For example, in chapter 8 one reads:

All of them, problematical ambiguous women, and other thousands and thousands of women frivolous and superficial in appearance, but honorable at heart most of them, solidly virtuous and sensible many of them, greeted the illustrious rogue (Currita) as she passed by, bowing to her, rendering her the homage of their smiles and their envy, making themselves guilty of that pernicious tolerance of vice, that mortal wound of great societies. These women were contributing with their presence and their satisfaction, through foolishness, through weakness, or through malice, to the great sin of scandal, to the triumph of the most vile scoundrel who ever plotted an intrigue at court.

This statement, which contains the thesis of *Bagatelles,* is to be found side by side with the narrator's fine description of the demonstration of mantillas and *peinetas* and its breakup by the pimp and prostitutes. Thus the reader has before him a novel with some fine characterization (that of Currita and Diogenes, for example) and some interesting history, and also occasional comments showing discontent with the characters and the history. The discontented being is not the novelist, who obviously likes what he is doing, but the missionary, who does not like what he sees. Fortunately for the reader of *Bagatelles,* the novelist is often unmindful of the missionary's existence; he takes pleasure in the story he is writing and is carried away by it; he enjoys creating a com-

ico-serious scene about an awkward minister and rascally woman and a
fireplace on 25 June, and a *commedia dell'arte* scene about a doltish
aristocrat, a melon, asking a drunken cynic the meaning of a ridiculous
Latin word. The preaching of the missionary cannot destroy these
works of art.

Book 1, Chapters 10–11

Chapters 10 and 11 turn to a thesis against dueling and to melo-
drama. Currita has been offended by an article in the newspaper *Spain
with Honor* and she demands that her *protégé* Juanito Velarde challenge
the editor to a duel. Juanito does as he is told and at dawn, in a distant
forest, despite the dictates of his conscience and religion, he exchanges
shots with a frightened editor. He is killed. The duel has ended in
three bagatelles: a desolate mother, a soul in hell, and a new fashion
in clothing introduced by Currita, who, half mourning, wears a black
glove on one hand and a white glove on the other.

Chapter 10 begins with a sentenious saying: "It has been said that
hypocrisy is a homage vice renders to virtue, and it is equally certain
that the false idea of honor is a reverence that scoundrels make to good
men, who are slaves of true honor." In the sentence following the one
just cited the repeated use of "the latter . . . the former . . . the former
. . . the latter" creates confusion: one of the accusations of Coloma's
critics has been his slovenly writing. The sentenious style continues:
"There are persons who suffer from a sort of moral strabismus, which
makes them see the thin where there's fat, and the fat where only the
thin exists." This saying applies especially to Villamelón, for whom
the corruption of society is only a bagatelle. His honor as a husband is
at stake, but he concerns himself with a pane in a French window,
broken in a door the day of the police search.

Chapter 10 ends with Juanito Velarde's remembering his mother and
the catechism he was taught as a child. Good and evil are polarized:
there is heaven and hell, the Virgin of the Rule and the world, flesh
and devil; and Juanito's mother on the one hand and Currita on the
other. He chooses unwisely and goes to hell. This scene, with its flash-
back dialogue, exclamation marks, and interrogations reads like a
drama, bringing to mind Manuel Tamayo y Baus's famous thesis play,
Duels of Honor (1863). One event recalls Tamayo's other melodramas,
namely, Velarde's purchase of a lottery ticket, which wins 15,000 *duros*
after his death. "¡Extraña burla de la suerte!" (Strange mockery of fate!)

The money comes into Currita's hands, whose ultimate disposition of it shows her base character and the nobility of Juanito's mother. Book 1 ends with bitter irony:

On seeing that the long train of problems Butrón had prophesied when she was named lady-in-waiting was cut off once and for all thanks to her own efforts, Currita could now breathe freely. The political consequences were clear, producing among other results three different *bagatelles*:

> A desolate mother.
> A soul in hell.
> And the fashion of different-colored gloves.

Meanwhile, Villamelón was zealously preparing the photographs from which the pictures would be taken for the *Illustrated Review*; everything else he had thrown in that drawer of his labeled *Byzantine Questions*.

In this passage the narrator himself italicizes *bagatelles* (*pequeñeces*), thus underlining the sarcasm of the novel's title, as if it said: "you, the aristocracy, call maternity and salvation bagatelles, ranking them with a scoundrel's wearing two different gloves, whereas they are not, and you may join Velarde in hell for your attitude!" As for Villamelón, the hair-splitting questions he calls *Byzantine* include a dueler's death and his own cuckoldry.

Book 2, Chapters 1–4

In book 2 the scene of *Bagatelles* moves to the Grand Hotel in Paris, in February 1873, where trainloads of Spanish aristocrats and *haute-bourgeoisie* have taken refuge after the abdication of King Amadeo. The future is unpredictable! One hears rumors of carnage in Madrid! Bloodshed! And indeed blood has been spilled, for the "voluminous" Mrs. López Moreno arrives with a torn ear lobe, a wound she received on passing through Carlist territory where an unknown hand reached into the stage and snatched one of her five hundred ducat earrings. Diogenes, who is on hand to receive all the Spanish aristocrats coming to Paris, reserves his fiercest barbs for the social-climbing Mrs. López Moreno. Her banker husband has gone to Matapuerca (Killsow) in Extremadura to look after the estate they acquired when Mendizábal confiscated church lands (1837):

"He's in Matapuerca . . . if he's alive. . . !"

"In Matapuerca," exclaimed Diogenes. "It can't be! . . . He must be in Matapuerco (Killhog)."

"No, no, in Matapuerca," replied López Moreno's wife without understanding the old man's cutting remark.

Currita Albornoz declares that it is delightful "to hear Mrs. López Moreno describe the *dégringolade* of Matapuerca." Within this farce set in the Grand Hotel of Paris, the narrator tells a serious story. Juxtaposing the profound and the superficial, the grave and the ridiculous, and intervening only occasionally with his parenthetical statements, he creates some of the best chapters in *Bagatelles*.

Jacobo Téllez-Ponce, Marquis of Sabadell, has come to Paris from Marseilles with the aplomb of a seasoned traveler. Riding a coach through the city, he looks at none of the sights but meditates on the past and on the portfolio in his hand addressed to King Amadeo. He has led a wasteful life and now, past thirty, he must try to set his house in order. He is somehow associated with the assassination of General Prim, the architect of Amadeo's regime, and with two more assassinations in Constantinople, where he served as minister plenipotentiary. The portfolio contains three documents bearing the seal of the Masons. Should he return them to the Italian lodges or use them for his own purposes? Fate decides his future action in the person of the effeminate *fantoche* (puppet), Tío Frasquito:

Glued, dyed, combed, and glossy by dint of cosmetics, and dancing on the tips of his toes, since his very tight hose allowed him no other mode of walking although it failed to hide two fabled bunions, Uncle Frasquito hastily went out on the terrace, he the universal uncle of the Grandees of Spain, and of those their adjutants the nobles of second rank, of the vulgar rich of every cast, of political and literary notabilities, of official loafers, of daring adventurers and anonymous personages who form the *all Madrid* of the Court, the ill-matched *dessus du panier* of the great Madrilenian world.

Tío Frasquito has a tight corset shielding "the insolent mutinies of his abdomen," and legend has it that he carries in his body thirty-two prosthetic parts, the most legendary of which is one of his buttocks, made of cork. He has a complete set of false teeth, save one, manufactured for ten thousand francs by Mr. Ernest, Napoleon III's famous dentist. He wears a perfumed wig. His manners are those of a modest maiden, the cadences of his voice, of a vain lady. He pronounces Span-

ish with a French *r*: "De la Rrrepública española! . . . Córrrdoba, se-
ñores, Córrrdoba! . . . ¡Ferrrnandito Córrrdoba, rrrepublicano! . . .
¡Quién lo creyerra! . . ." Frasquito also has an implacable enemy, the
crapulous Diogenes, who embarrasses him at every opportunity: "Diogenes usually called him *Francesca di Rimini*, at times *señá Frasquita,*
and he pursued him and accosted him through sitting rooms and living
rooms even among the skirts of the ladies, where the effeminate great
man was wont to take refuge, showering him with untimely embraces
that wrinkled and soiled his immaculate shirt front." Diogenes constantly tries to discover the thirty-two prosthetic components "assigned
to his body by legend."

At this point the person behind the narrator intervenes in the story.
Although the intervention is not as blunt as in Coloma's earlier stories,
the reader nevertheless realizes he is reading a thesis novel; the terrible
example of Frasquito and Diogenes is spelled out for him: "Those two
old men, of characters and customs so diverse, were, however, two
stragglers of the same society, two exemplary fossils of those celebrities
of the last century, vicious and cynical toughs some of them, fops,
superficialities and effeminates the others, who paved the way in Spain
for the ruin and discredit of the Grandees."[2]

In chapter 4 Jacobo, the former Mason dealing in blackmail and
international intrigue, meets Frasquito in his hotel room in the most
ridiculous circumstance: the tassel of the old fool's nightcap is on fire.
The narrator writes:

The little door was then opened violently and Jacobo appeared, revolver in
hand. . . . It was impossible to recognize Tío Frasquito in that scarecrow, and
Jacobo didn't realize who he was until the phantasm, rushing up to him with
open arms, shouted in anguish: "Jacobo! . . . Jacobo!" . . . The latter, not
understanding what was going on yet, first tried him with a big slap on the
head, and the burning cap fell on the ground, revealing a perfectly bare skull,
white and shiny like a winter melon. All of that was a grotesque scene from
a farce, taking place in a second, and nevertheless that small and ridiculous
triviality of life decided forever the fate of Jacobo. . . .

The words "scarecrow" (*esperpento*) and "grotesque scene from a farce"
("grotesca escena de sainete") provide a further key to the art of *Bagatelles.* The writer here is not the missionary-novelist, but only the novelist proclaiming that his satirical art is one of systematic deformation.[3]

To return to the plot: Tío Frasquito is a renowned collector of seals, and in Jacobo's room on seeing the Masonic imprint in wax he expresses a great interest in it. On the spur of the moment, "burning his ships," Jacobo delivers three seals to him, an act resulting in the assassination scene of book 4 and the ultimate conversion of Currita. The comico-serious plot is unusual but not implausible.

Book 2, Chapters 5–8

The second half of book 2 takes leave of Paris and "the Columbine simplicity" of Currita Albornoz for Biarritz and an interview between the shameless Marquis of Sabadell (Jacobo) and the virtuous Marchioness of Villasis. It begins with a low comedy equivocation in which Villamelón keeps calling Jacobo *Benito* and ends with diplomatic swordplay, the victor being María Villasis, "the asute Antonelli," and the loser Jacobo Sabadell, "Mr. Bismarck." Ultramontanist piety carries the day over worldly *Realpolitik.*

The author's thesis is rather subtly presented here. Instead of doctrinal broadsides one comes upon a passage such as this:

The whim of a queen quickly converted a forgotten little village into one of the most fashionable centers of the demigods who regulate customs, luxury, necessities and even conscience. . . .[4] The empress Eugenia built in Biarritz the *ville Eugénie,* and Biarritz arrived at the level of Trouville, Dieppe, and Etretat. The Spaniards invade it in summer, the English in winter, the Russians in autumn, as if they wanted to take turns enjoying its quite problematical comforts and its very questionable charms.

Luxurious wealth hastened to build there *villas* and palaces; speculation, hotels and casinos; only piety failed to raise a hand. In Biarritz there scarcely exists a church.

There is scarcely a church, and so there must be many scoundrels. At Biarritz two saintly women like Elvira Sabadell and María Villasis are roses among thorns.

In chapter 7 one again detects Coloma behind the narrator, writing *pro domo sua*: "Jacobo had presented himself [to Father Cifuentes] concealing, behind his arrogant haughtiness, the awkwardness and the sort of suspicious fear that Jesuits customarily instil in worldly persons who know them only from the thousands of false stories that circulate in writing or by word of mouth, favoring them or condemning them."[5] At the end of chapter 6 the narrator advances the action: Diogenes sends a letter to María Villasis warning her that Jacobo is coming to Biarritz to take advantage of his wealthy wife, whom he has not seen in ten years. In a postscript the crapulous old cynic also reveals a tenderness for María's granddaughter, Monina. The passage is plausible and facilitates his death-bed repentance in book 4; thus there is no deus ex machina scene as there might have been in Coloma's stories.

Bagatelles is sprinkled with literary allusions, which convey the cosmopolitan atmosphere of upper-class Madrilenians in the nineteenth century. Some allusions are not immediately recognizable, apparently being ironic references to romantic and sentimental novels of the author's day. Others are better known, for example, a comparison of Sabadell to the donjuanesque Mañara. Others are universally known or revealed to the reader by the narrator:

And here Jacobo seemed very moved, and gave evidence of his erudition, reciting from memory the lines of Dante:

> Nessun maggior dolore
> Che ricordarsi del tempo felice
> Nella miseria

and paraphrasing it with those other lines from the Marquis of Santillana:

> La mayor cuyta que aver
> Puede ningún amador,
> Es membrarse del placer
> En el tiempo del dolor.[6]

Jacobo the prevaricator employs these verses for a nefarious end, the abuse of his wife and her fortune. Ironically, lying he tells the truth, for the poetry of Dante and the Marquis of Santillana most suitably describe his own condition.

The many literary allusions suggest a strange ambivalence in *Bagatelles,* which at times strikes the reader as a novel mixing humanism and a sort of Spanish Catholic fundamentalism. On the one hand, the style of the book is open and European, allowing for French, Spanish, Italian, English, Latin, German, and Greek literature, for history, for irony, caricature, low comedy, and an *esperpento*; whereas on the other hand the thesis of the book, while condemning scandalous *bagatelles* that are not really trivia, is excessively demanding and closed in its political science and ethics. It argues for a kind of Ptolemaic society in which revolution per se is the work of traitors, and certain institutions, the altar and the throne, are irrevocably fixed and may not be changed. Ethically, it asks for a social system of "fumigation and isolation," by which ladies like María Villasis would invite only "honorable men and decent women to their homes."

In defense of *Bagatelles,* let it be said that the customs of Madrilenian high society were probably not admirable;[7] but the doctrine of isolation urged by María Villasis in this thesis novel is difficult and perhaps impossible of attainment. One can always isolate oneself and an occasional public malefactor, but it would require a divine scrutiny to categorize all human beings as honorable or dishonorable. Perhaps the ambivalence of *Bagatelles* will account for its unusual acceptance. Frequently criticized as a poor novel, it is still being read and still being printed. The thesis is divisive; the style is not, or at least the style of Coloma the novelist as opposed to Coloma the missionary-novelist. One may reject the political philosophy and the ethics, but not the figures of Frasquito, Villamelón, Currita, and Diogenes set against the historical background of Restoration Spain.

Book 3

In his study published during the *Bagatelles* tumult of 1891, Emilio Bobadilla makes an interesting observation: "Even in the comic, picaresque note, with which most of the chapters in *Bagatelles* end, I find a likeness between Alarcón and Coloma. Recall, for example, the extremely witty scenes of *The Three Cornered Hat* and *Bagatelles.* For the truth is that in P. Coloma as in Alarcón, the satirical tendency dominates."[8] Using Bobadilla's remark as a guide, a study of the eight chapters in book 3 will illuminate the nature of Coloma's art.

Five chapters (1–2, 4, 6–7) end humorously, the humor ranging from a smile to wry scorn. Villamelón asks Diogenes what he does for a cold, and the cynic replies: "Snore . . ." (1); one duchess, thinking of a charity ball, wonders what the dress of the parvenue Mrs. Martínez will be like—perhaps like that of Teresa Panza, Sancho's wife (2); Diogenes is not surprised at Villamelón's interest in the artificial incubation of eggs, because "Está clueco" (he is broody; *clueco* is applied not only to hens but also to old, debilitated people [4]); at a women's congress, with two hundred great ladies present, "the respectable Marquis of Butrón," alias Robinson Crusoe, his man Friday, Mr. Pulido, and Tío Frasquito are crouching on the floor behind a curtain, spying on them, when Diogenes pulls a cord raising the curtain (6); and a French courtesan, Mademoiselle Sirop, whose fondness for camelias has won her the nickname of the *dama de las camelias,* sends Currita a silver picture frame as a gift for "the wounded soldiers of the North." It bears the inscription: "To the Most Excellent Señora Condesa de Albornoz." The frame is an heirloom of Currita's family, given to the lady of the camelias by one of Currita's lovers, Jacobo Sabadell (7).

Chapters 3, 5, and 8 end seriously. In chapter 3 Jacobo hurls Currita's young son to the ground, where he strikes his head and spills blood; in chapter 5 the saintly wife of Butrón must ask the virtuous Marchioness of Villasis to attend a scandalous gathering; and in chapter 8 Jacobo leaves Madrid to justify his conduct before Garibaldi and the Masonic lodges of Italy. Thus Coloma alternates comic scenes with drama, the former serving as relief for the latter. The comedy ridicules what is vicious whereas the drama falls on vicious and virtuous alike. Innocent schoolboys will perish because of high society's scandalous *bagatelles,* and so will the renegade Mason, Jacobo Sabadell.

In book 3 Coloma's humor becomes as scabrous perhaps as a nineteenth-century reading public will allow. In one scene Villamelón's young son inexpertly paints his father's portrait, so that two locks of hair resemble two horns; Jacobo laughs at the picture and chalks in the horns in Currita's presence. In another scene Diogenes asks Currita for a ride in her coach, but she does not want to accommodate him. He then cuts her down with a scathing remark:

"But, woman, you're passing by right where I want to go. . . . You just leave me on Alcalá Street, at the chocolate shop of Doña Mariquita. . . . I wouldn't give up my hot toddy with its pair of sweet buns for anything in the world. . . ."
"They are delicious," observed Villamelón.
"How delightful!," said Currita. "If they gave them to you right in the teeth every night, perhaps you wouldn't have such a long tongue."
"Shoot! . . . If they gave them to you right in the I know where, maybe you wouldn't give people so many grounds for gossiping about you."
Currita bit her lip realizing it was impossible to fight with that savage.

These lines come from the pen of a novelist, not a missionary. Similar humor is found in a story like Coloma's *La Gorriona,* where an innocent woman unwittingly plays the part of a procuress.

One other joke of book 3, this one at the expense of the self-serving Marquis of Butrón, deserves mention here. Butrón had received an inscribed photograph of Queen Victoria:

But her gracious majesty undoubtedly did not handle the language of Cervantes with great art, and intending to write in keeping with the English construction, *Al marqués de Butrón, recuerdo,* she forgot to put in the *u,* and there resulted, *Al marqués de Butrón, recerdo* signed and sealed with the hand and letter of her gracious majesty, sovereign of three united kingdoms and Empress of India.

In Spanish, *recuerdo* means *regards* or *in memory,* whereas *recerdo* means *big pig*: "To the Marquis of Butrón, big pig," Signed, Victoria. The narrator of *Bagatelles* is an incorrigible humorist.[9]

In all the corroding humor of book 3 two ideas stand out: (1) scandalous conduct is not a bagatelle, and (2) Jacobo, Marquis of Sabadell, must face the Masons, who are allied with Satan. Whereas a scandalous woman like Currita belongs to the phenomenal world, the dark power of the Masons is something metaphysical, archangelic, reaching into a realm beyond the scope of the senses. The Masons, who are occasionally suggested or mentioned in the early books, will make their appearance in book 4.

Book 4

Historically, book 4 takes up the events following 29 December 1874, when General Martínez Campos proclaimed Prince Alfonso, son of Isabel II, king of Spain. The Restoration was accomplished, and the nation no longer had to preoccupy itself with foreign pretenders, republics, anarchy, or "Spain without a King." The one remaining obstacle was the Carlist civil war, in which destiny favored the throne of the new young monarch, Alfonso XII. Beyond history, however, there lay a sort of antinomic struggle, a war that loomed large in the mind of Luis Coloma and his contemporaries: indeed, book 4 of *Bagatelles* may be called "the book of the Masons."

Of the nine chapters in book 4 and the epilogue, only chapter 3 has a Colomesque comic ending, and a mild one at that. The book begins with a wonderful scene of Currita driving a coach wildly through the countryside with her irresponsible friends on board, but its whole tone is eschatological: the cynical, crapulous Diogenes dies well shriven; an old Jesuit, a former friend and teacher of Diogenes, dies in the odor of sanctity; Jacobo Sabadell dies, unrepentant and unshriven, his fate recalling the death of Juan Velarde in book 1; and the two young boys, Paquito and Tapón, are drowned in a rip tide, innocent victims of society's bagatelles, their death evoking the Virgin of Recollection in the opening chapter of the novel. None of these deaths are implausible, and lest they seem excessive in a brief description such as this, let it be said that book 4 resembles Fernando de Rojas's *La Celestina*. The *celestina,* the procuress, is a scandalous society, and the result of her ironic bagatelles is death and, in some cases, damnation. In Coloma's story "La Gorriona," which resembles *Bagatelles,* one can also see the similarity to *La Celestina.*

The central chapters, 5 and 6, end with the image of blood:

> meanwhile Jacobo opened the message. On a sheet of white paper he could see the distinctive red seal that had been previously stamped on the envelope of the Masonic documents. He looked at it for a moment, terrified. It looked to him like a drop of blood. (chapter 5)

> [These words appear after the murder of Jacobo, which Currita had witnessed.] In the light of that lamp Currita looked at her hands, which felt wet and sticky, and she saw them stained with blood. . . . An immense horror invaded her body and overwhelmed her soul, and one idea at least pierced her mind, like a nail burning at the blow of a mallet; that of her daughter Lilí, kneeling in the study, showing her little hands stained also in the blood of her brother, repeating with the opaque vibration of a boundless terror: "Blood! . . . Mama . . . Blood!" (chapter 6)

The Masons connote personal evil, like the giant angel Lucifer, whom every man must contend with in his journey through life. The manifold evils in the book—the death of General Prim (whose assassination in 1870 resembles that of Jacobo Sabadell in 1875); the Revolution of 1868; the machinations of Garibaldi and the Italian lodges; the uncanny night of Carnival; the opposition to the altar and the throne; the secret messages; the stealing of the seals given to Frasquito; the murders of Velarde and Jacobo; the deaths of Diogenes, the two boys, and a holy priest; and perhaps even the amorous scandals of Madrid—may somehow or other be attributed to the Masons, who are omnipresent. They are everywhere, endeavoring to spoil the Edenic scene of book 1, chapter 1.

This vision of the Masons, equating their powers with those of Satan, faithfully portrays the climate of Coloma's day. The historian Vicente de la Fuente, whose book appeared in 1881, just ten years before the publication of *Bagatelles,* attributes to the Masons every successful and attempted assassination of the nineteenth century. De la Fuente writes:

I have tried to tell the truth and to be impartial, an extremely difficult thing. I declare I have had no fear at all in writing it; but my friends and relatives have taken charge of being afraid for me. No enemy has made me the slightest threat, and in spite of the fact that it was well known that I was gathering documents and data for this work, no Freemason, *comunero,* or *carbonario* has taken the slightest trouble to oppose my work or to intimidate me. My friends tell me it is still too early to judge, and they dream of daggers, persecutions, poisons, loss of my university chair, lawsuits, denunciations, charges of calumny, and I don't know how many things else, and they prophesy for me the sad ending of Riera y Comas, who they say died as an emigré, persecuted and poisoned because of his novel, *The Mysteries of the Secret Societies.*[10]

Vincente de la Fuente is not as impartial as he sincerely believes himself to be, but he is truthful. The same statement may be predicated of the author of *Bagatelles.* And whatever other virtues or defects this novel may have, it gives the reader a true picture of the subjective fears, conspiratorial fears, of the nineteenth century. Perhaps Luis Coloma would say that the fears were not subjective but founded in metaphysical reality, since the Masonic lodges were temples of Beelzebub.

The conspiratorial fears of the day were not restricted to an allegedly Christian or Jesuitical work like *Bagatelles*; it was also to be found in the books of opponents of the church or Jesuits, for example, the novels of Vicente Blasco Ibáñez. The Jesuits for Blasco Ibáñez play the same role as the Masons for Father Coloma: they are the disciples of Beelzebub. In Blasco's long novel, *The Black Spider,* this derogatory metaphor is his symbol for the Jesuit order. He divided his novel into ten parts, the first three of which will be discussed here: "El conde de Baselga" (Count Baselga); "El padre Claudio" (Father Claudio); and "El señor Avellaneda" (Mr. Avellaneda).[11] In the first part of these novels Baselga marries a Mexican woman, who delivers a child he believes to be his own, but really is the bastard of the cruel king, Ferdinand VII. Although the Jesuit superior, Father Claudio, knows this, he cruelly and cynically encourages the marriage to further the order's control in Spain. In the second book a furious Baselga strangles his wife. Father

Claudio covers everything up because the order can use Baselga in the future. The third book moves to Paris, where a forty-year-old Baselga wants to marry the beautiful María Avellaneda, a union the Jesuits hope to prevent since they want to inherit the young girl's fifteen million francs. The Jesuits always wear filthy (*mugriento*) garments and peculiar smiles (*sonrisa de los jesuitas*), the equivalent of Coloma's mudhole (*lodazal*) and dirty pool (*charca cenagosa*).

In an archetypal sense the Jesuit Luis Coloma and the anti-Jesuit Blasco Ibáñez are writing the same novel. Both men see Innocence in an Edenic state threatened by a serpent, the Enemy. Both authors create narrators who on occasion intervene and profess to know everything; these narrators will not hesitate to use a rhetoric of assertion. Both of them are writing thesis novels. When it comes to filling in the detail of their air maps, the Jesuit and anti-Jesuit part ways. For Coloma, Christian souls, illuminated by supernatural love, are attacked by the world, the flesh, and the devil, incarnate in the ubiquitous Masons, whereas for Blasco Ibáñez, young people, illuminated by natural love, are attacked by the Jesuits, "the gigantic black spider that proposes to take the whole world into its web." There was a great deal of conspiratorial fear in the nineteenth century, on all sides. [12]

Book 4 of *Bagatelles* will show that Luis Coloma had drunk deeply at the wells of nineteenth-century positivism. Chapter 4 pits the virtuous Marchioness, María Villasis, against the scandalous Countess, Currita Albornoz. Both hold a soirée on the same night of the week, and Currita notices defections in the ranks; whereas there used to be twenty guests at her table, there are now seven *bajas* (drops), and so only thirteen to sup with her. María Villasis, representing virtue, has won by a sort of football score, 20–13. The same numerical rationale (proof by positive numbers) holds in other cases also. María Villasis, by a practical doctrine of "isolation and fumigation" ("aislamiento y fumigación") invites to her house only "honorable women and decent men"; at one juncture there are 120 women invited and only fourteen excluded, among them of course Currita, with the narrator concluding that Madrid is not such a mudhole (*lodazal*) after all. How does he know? The score tells him: 120–14.

In addition to arithmetical proofs such as these, the author, Coloma, intervenes in his novel occasionally with a footnote to offer historical proof. There are seventeen such footnotes in all of *Bagatelles* performing the following tasks: translating lines from Basque, Turkish, or English; explaining Father Nieremberg's use of the *disciplina*; declaring that a passage about the opera paraphrases Peña y Goñi's review of *Dinorah* in a journal; quoting an authentic last will and testament; or telling the origin of some verses. One author's note seeks to prove historically an event that is not strictly provable, the timely death of Father Mateu, who was preserved by the Lord until he could confess the dying Diogenes: "The death of this saintly old man, which took place at the same time as that of the person he was aiding, is a strictly historical fact" (book 4, chapter 2). There is no reason to doubt the author's veracity. The death itself is indeed historical, but its timing by divine providence belongs rather to the realm of faith. The canons of positivism do not operate here. Four of Coloma's footnotes, protesting that *Bagatelles* is not a *novela de clave*, will excite the reader's sympathy (see Benítez's edition of *Bagatelles*, pages 88, 189, 284, 414). He was upset by the accusations made against him.

Conversion

Although *Bagatelles* contains the melodramatic polarization of virtue versus vice, the conversions of Diogenes and Currita are not implausible. The old cynic's character is so developed in the novel as to permit the entrance of grace, and Currita's conversion is gradual rather than sudden. She has received the letter from the Jesuit superior offending her vanity, she has been humbled by *la Villasis* in their social duel, she was at Jacobo's side when he was stabbed in the aorta by the Masons, and she has lost her son in the rip tide before coming to terms with the almighty. Coloma's contemporaries may not have cared for this spiritual solution, but their objections to Currita's conversion are questionable.

The Style of *Bagatelles*

During and after the *Bagatelles* debate of 1891, Coloma was accused of many offenses against the Spanish language and grammar: the excessive use of neologisms and foreign words, careless assonance, amphibology, cacophony, and certain "inaccuracies and errors"—for example, the confusion of "spheres" with "circles" and of "lintels" (*dinteles*), with "thresholds" (*umbrales*).[13] Some critics, perhaps not distinguishing between style and content, would not forgive him any of his linguistic transgressions, whereas others came to his support arguing that these transgressions "were punishable by the laws of grammar but not by those of rhetoric,"[14] for although his prose abounds in neologisms, it is "transparent and animated, flexible and picturesque."[15] But all the critics, friend and foe, agreed that his prose was unpolished. The most egregious of Coloma's linguistic faults is his writing in assonance. The Spanish language is more given to assonant rhyme (the rhyming of the vowels but not the consonants in the stressed syllables of words) than English because of its verb inflection, gender, and the vast number of words ending in vowels; for example, *placa, estrada, gafa, baja, mala, llana, mapa, masa, mata, plaza, playa, palma, bisagra, lava, llama* (present indicative, third person, first conjugation), *llamaba* (imperfect indicative), *llamara* (imperfect subjunctive), and *llamada* (past participle used as a feminine adjective) all rhyme in assonance, *a-a*. It follows that the Spanish prose writer must take care to avoid unintentional rhyming and the stress associated with rhyme, which might prove awkward or even comical. Luis Coloma, as the following examples will show, did not listen to his own prose and so he frequently wrote sentences with repeated assonance: "sin que levantase *ella* la *cabeza* ni *hiciera* un movimiento, como si la *vergüenza* de su vida *entera* la tuviese allí *sujeta, clavada* ante las *miradas* . . ." (six of these twenty-six words rhyme in assonant *e-a*, and two of the last four words in *a-a*); "Currita abrió la gran *tapa* delantera, cuyas *bisagras* y *cerrajas doradas dejaban* . . ." (*a-a*); "*abajo* un gran *paño* de *brocado recamado* . . ." (*a-o*; there is also consonance in *-ado*); "A través de sus *largas pestañas, extrañada* . . ." (*a-a*); "Y ambos *echaron* a andar *agarrados* del *brazo, atravesando* . . ." (*a-o*); "de *seda* y encajes *crema,* a la *bella Condesa* . . ." (*e-a*); "del poético *lago* o del *dramático Tajo,* un *trancazo soberano* . . ." (*a-o*). Sometimes the rhyme changes to pure consonance: "Lanzóse el *Gobernador* sobre ellos con todo el *ardor,* de su picado *amor* . . ."; "el plato *favorito,* del buen *Juanito* . . ."; "su humor *chancero,* tiróle a la mujer, lo *primero* . . ."; "un escándalo *iniciado* y *meditado* en casa de Currita, y *llevado* . . ."; "*cualquiera hubiera* creído. . . ." One critic of Coloma's day made a long list of such rhymes taken at random from *Bagatelles* and wittily pointed out that they sound at times like a cantabile and at others like a *cencerrada* (the noisy serenade of bells and horns on a widower's second wedding night).[16]

The other faults or unusual features of Coloma's prose are perhaps not so prominent as the assonant phrases, but taken together they make for an unpolished style. He is tautological, as in the phrase "a todas horas la moral divina de Dios . . ." (at all times the divine morality of God . . .); he is apt to write the popular *debistes* and *distes* rather than *debiste* and *diste*; he drops an *h*: "le había traído allí y échole aguantar con paciencia" (the *echo* should read *hecho*); he uses gallicisms, *revancha* for *desquite*, *avalancha* for *alud*, *pretencioso* for *presuntuoso*, "era el académico *en cuestión*" (many of these gallicisms have since come into common usage); he introduces feminine endings to words such as *intrigante, reo,* and *Quijote,* writing *la intriganta, la rea, una Quijota*; he leaves present participles dangling, without a clear antecedent; he changes the gender of a word: "Era un abanico muy bonito, de nácar quemada . . ." (instead of *nácar quemado*); his use of pejoratives like *fango, ciénaga, gusano asqueroso* (mud, quagmire, swamp, filthy worm)[17] is excessive; and his sentences often contain ambiguities because of their uncertain grammatical construction: "Porque su esposa prolongó su estirpe añadiéndole un niño y una niña, y la renta de él, según su frase . . ." (Because his wife extended *su* lineage by adding a son and a daughter, and his income, according to *su* statement . . .). It is difficult to ascertain here whose statement and even whose lineage is being referred to.

Coloma's most severe linguistic critic was Emilio Bobadilla (pen name, Fray Candil), who wrote some twenty-three pages concerning the imperfections of *Bagatelles.* Bobadilla concludes that there are limits to simplicity and naturalness, that in newspaper articles one can forgive some infractions of the rules owing to the haste they are written in, but "in a novel, and in a novel like *Bagatelles,* written in the retirement of a cloister, with all its tranquillity, such incorrectness, which if far from being minute, merits no indulgence."[18] On the other hand, the critic Federico Balart wrote: "The book is written *sans façon*: in the loose, natural, and hardly polished style of a talented man of the world who is editing his memoirs for the private use of his family. That carelessness, which rarely borders on slovenliness, will be for some the principal defect of the work; for me it contains one of its principal attractions."[19] The present writer will agree with Balart. Although the imperfections of *Bagatelles* are undeniable and do not merit indulgence as such, they nonetheless point to the principal charm of the book. Luis Coloma had a story to tell about an aristocratic society that was scandalizing the young and about a Restoration he deplored, and he told it quickly, clearly, and carelessly, so much so that he committed the same mistakes people make when they speak. *Bagatelles* is the saga of the Spanish Restoration, and its bard, for all his education and sacerdotal character, is just a provincial from Andalusia. Neither sophisticated nor broad-minded, he nevertheless knows how to tell a tale.[20]

The *Bagatelles* Affair: The *Algarada*

The Arabic word *algarada,* which means the din, uproar, and shouting made by a body of marauders, is akin to *algazara,* a Moorish war cry. These words were used in the Madrid of 1891 to describe the reception given to *Bagatelles* upon its publication, and one famous critic wrote a chapter on "The Whys of the Algarada."[21] If the reader will imagine a cavalry of Moslems and Christians screaming the names of Allah and St. James upon entering battle, he will have a good idea of how Coloma's novel was received. *Bagatelles* first ran as a serial novel in the *Sacred Heart Messenger* from January 1890 to March 1891 where it apparently elicited comment but nothing compared to the furor that was to follow. In the *Messenger* of January 1891 Coloma found it necessary to add a note saying: "Our characters are not portraits of certain specific individuals but rather broad social types. . . ."

There was some feeling that *Bagatelles* was a *novela de clave,* a novel in which the characters are real persons thinly disguised, but that feeling was still vague and indistinct. In March 1891 the book itself appeared and the critics were immediately heard from. Emilia Pardo Bazán praised the novel, but her favorable review was followed by a mounting wave of adverse criticism: Coloma was a Carlist and his book Jesuit propaganda, a libel, an attack on the aristocracy and Restoration. The criticism became so intense that from 2 April to 16 April the *Madrid Heraldo* opened its pages for a public airing of the question: any member of the reading public could write in offering his opinion of *Bagatelles.* The book became so widely read and criticism of it so popular that works criticizing it themselves became best-sellers; for example, M. Martínez Barrionuevo's sixty-page opuscule *An Unfortunate Book (Bagatelles of Father Coloma)* went through eight printings, and in the preface to his *Father Coloma and the Aristocracy* Emilio Bobadilla, explaining that he has written his book in great haste, jokingly has his publisher say to him: "Hurry up—he told me, as a midwife might say to a woman giving birth—for once the opportunity is gone, goodbye to my money!"[22] Those interested in the criticism surrounding the *Bagatelles* affair might consult the works of Federico Balart, Emilio Bobadilla, M. Martínez Barrionuevo, Emilia Pardo Bazán, and Juan Valera. They are listed and described in the bibliography.

We shall now turn to Coloma's other novel, *Boy,* which was his *hijo predilecto* (favorite son).

Chapter Four
The Other Novel: *Boy*
The Plot

The novel tells the story of two young aristocrats, Paco Marquis of Burunda and Boy Count of Baza. After many years of separation they meet at a masked ball, where Boy is escorting a beautiful lady whom Paco does not know. Later that night Paco and Boy take a stroll through the city ending at Paco's house, and still later a repugnant usurer is murdered. In the morning Paco is amazed to see that Boy's bed is empty.

As the evidence accumulates, it becomes apparent to many that Boy has committed the crime, and his continued absence aggravates his situation. When he returns to Paco's house and steadfastly refuses to give an alibi Paco is bewildered, but then he realizes Boy is protecting someone. But who?—the beautiful lady at the ball. Finally Boy flees, poses as a foreigner in the North, and enlists in the Carlist civil war where he is killed and his cadaver horribly mutilated. His name is cleared when the murderers are apprehended, and Paco closes the narration with a tribute to his friend.

Chapter 1 of *Boy*

The novel begins retrospectively. The narrator is Paco, whose theme is memory: "Boy . . . ! Twenty-five years have gone by since that meeting, the first prelude to an awful history of blood and tears, and I still recall the deepest joy with which that dear name sprung forth from my soul . . . Boy! . . ." Paco's memory returns to Shrove Monday in the spring of 1869, in Andalusia, when the September Revolution was still in the air:

I arrived at the ball at ten fifteen, when the entrance of the political personage being honored began to excite the crowd. He went through the large drawing rooms and the wide and sumptuous galleries, guided by General Belluga, who played the role of cicerone and presented him to the provincial celebrities. Behind him came the "personagess," with the displays and airs of a great lady of the ancient court, giving her arm to my uncle the duke of Sos, a traditional decorative figure in all the solemn public acts of the party of Isabel II; and, surrounded by young bucks and ladies, two "personagettes" took up the rear, daughters of the personage; the one a little brunette, picturesquely walleyed, the other a dull blonde with a little mouth of which Bussy might say what he said of "mademoiselle" Mancini:

> . . . that amorous little beak
> which runs from ear to ear.

In these opening lines of the novel Paco displays a wry mental ability to portray things in a twisted light. The reader has encountered this smiling astuteness before, in *Bagatelles,* when the *socarrón monarca* Ferdinand VII was baptizing Villamelón or the cynic Diogenes was witnessing the congress of ladies. Paco does not care for the nouveaux riches or the aristocrats who marry off their titled sons to the daughters of the newly rich, and he deprecates them with quotation marks, neologisms, diminutives, physical incongruities, and French verses, in a word, with all manner of irony. On the other hand, Paco admires the lordly nature of his friend Boy. Paco is a philo-aristocrat who knows that the true aristocracy, unlike the bourgeoisie, are very close to the spirit of Spain; hence he frequently quotes popular couplets, proverbs, and ballads (*romances*). When Boy, masked for the carnival ball, approaches Paco for the first time after many years, he sings verses to the sound of the *diana* (reveille) as if they were playing charades:

> Levántate, aspirante,
> que las cinco son,
> y viene el ayudante
> con su levitón.

> Get up, young cadet,
> the clock's at five,
> the adjutant comes
> with his frock coat fine.

And Paco remembers: "That reminder of my days in the Naval Academy aroused my curiosity, and I quickly removed the gloved hands from my eyes."

At the ball, Boy dressed as Pierrot is accompanied by a charming Pierrette, whose beautiful eyes pierce through her mask at Paco, and the latter recalls "a certain Andalusian couplet that spontaneously came to my memory":

> Anoche soñaba yo
> que dos negros me mataban,
> y eran tus hermosos ojos
> que enojados me miraban.

> Last night I was dreaming
> two blacks were killing me,
> and they were your eyes so fair
> which in fury looked at me.

Those two eyes will acquire importance in the murder accusation against Boy, but for the time being Paco's theme is memory, especially of his beautiful friend.

Within the broader scope of memory, Paco introduces the *topos* of *Et in Arcadia Ego* (And I, Death, in Arcadia).[1] At the ball he listens to the gossip of the Countess of Porrata, who declares that Boy is in the hands of the usurers, especially the vicious Joaquinito López, otherwise known as the Green Parrot. Boy has casually threatened López. Paco, believing her story, calls it a bad augury ("funestos augurios"), as indeed it is, for the morning after the ball the Green Parrot is found murdered. When Boy is accused of the crime and Paco tries to wrest his secret from him (where was he during the wee hours of that fateful morning?), he will say nothing. Half in jest, "with a note of sadness and bitterness that touched me to the soul," he begins to sing this Andalusian couplet:

> No tengo padre ni madre
> ni quién se acuerde de mí,
> me arrimo a los *mulaares*
> las moscas huyen de mí.

> I have no father or mother
> or someone to think of me,
> I take refuge in the dungheaps
> the flies they flee from me.

Whereas Paco had heard some gossip he considers to be an augury, the Green Parrot himself had had a premonition of death. On the evening of his murder he was heard to sing:

> Tin-tán
> a la puerta llaman
> Tin-tán
> yo no quiero abrir
> Tin-tán
> si será la muerte
> Tin-tán
> que vendrá por mí.

> Tin-tan
> there's a knock at the door
> Tin-tan
> I don't want to open
> Tin-tan
> lest it be death
> Tin-tan
> who will come for me.

The pairing of Arcadia (Paco's joyous memories of his youthful friendship with Boy) and Death continues throughout the novel until the last chapter (38).

Chapters 2–11

In Chapters 2–11 the narrator, Paco Burunda, develops his own character and that of Boy. Paco is a sentimental young man who wears his heart on his sleeve, whereas Boy has a "stoical pruritus" by which he is loathe to show emotion no matter how joyful or sorrowful the occasion may be: "Because I knew too well that all those boyish flippancies and impertinent witticisms were nothing else than the pruritus of Stoicism, an offspring of his self-esteem, which since his childhood made him conceal with studied frivolities the outbursts and feelings of his generous, sensitive, and even impressionable heart." The stoical character of Boy, the sentimental Victorian Spaniard who could not give vent to his feelings, is Coloma's finest novelistic achievement.

One brief paragraph of chapter 3, referring to a masked ball at carnival time, contains a description of the art of *Boy*: "I looked around, frightened, as I turned the corner of the hallway, and I remember this and I will remember it as long as I live, because it seemed to me that I saw there, in the flesh, one of those *caprichos* of Goya combining the ridiculous with the fantastic and even with the terrible, which leave in the soul a strange impression one could call comic fright." The novel *Boy* is like a *capricho* of Goya. The opening chapters reveal the horrible murder at carnival time of the Green Parrot, a hairdresser who is also a usurer: "The hairdresser was a hermaphroditic, effeminate type, a little old man, vile and repugnant, not for his untidiness but rather his excessive cleanliness. He still had a large thick head of hair, which was the pride of his arrogance and boast of his trade." Within its carnival atmosphere, moreover, the novel ridicules the affectations of the bourgeoisie.

Chapter 12

Chapter 12 introduces a change in the pace of the novel. There has been a crescendo in the action leading up to the murder of the Green Parrot and disappearance of Boy, but this chapter returns to the leisurely mnemonic movement of the opening chapters: Paco reminisces about his childhood friendship with the daughters of the judge now inquiring into the crime. The following chapter, 13, picks up the action again. One wonders why chapter 12 acts as a kind of caesura, inducing a new beginning or opening as it were. Perhaps there is an aesthetic reason, which the reader should indeed look for; nevertheless, the historian knows that there are external reasons for the interruption. The first eleven chapters of *Boy* appeared serially in the *Sacred Heart Messenger* of 1893, but after this date the superiors of the Jesuit order halted both the writing and publication of the remaining chapters of the novel. We do not know the reason for this, although it seems probable that the *Bagatelles* affair of 1891 had something to do with it. In any case, Coloma did not get to finish writing the novel until 1910, after a lapse of seventeen years, a break undoubtedly affecting the creation of *Boy*. The inspiration for a work of art, coming at a given time in a man's life, will brook no postponement. Coloma, who had taken a religious vow of obedience, felt he must obey his superiors; he stopped writing at their command and so sacrificed what would have been his finest artistic creation.[2]

The last sixteen chapters of the book tell the story of a young man, Boy, who yearns for his father's affections against the opposition of a ruthless stepmother. He faces another obstacle in his determination to save the honor of a married woman he has loved, she of the two black eyes in the poem mentioned above; and this leads him to his death in the Carlist civil war. Within the plot the reader's interest is held by several aspects of the novel: the couplets and other verses; the sententious sayings; the strange scene of Boy's father, living inside a stagecoach within his own house; the jokes; the airs of a *cursi,* unaristocratic stepmother ("She was tall and well formed, and in her youth she must have been one of those run-of-the-mill *good lasses* who can be found by the dozen at the market"—Paco the narrator reveals the same aristocratic bias as Coloma); a pun; social notes, such as the grandees' using the familiar *tú* when addressing one another; a definition of providence as "God writes straight with twisted lines"; Boy's concept of divine grace ("Atame, Señor, y ten piedad de mí"—"Bind me, Lord, and have mercy on me!"); but, above all, the characterization of Boy, the young aristocrat whose stoical pruritus prevents his accepting praise without a wry remark, or with a demonstration of emotion. In this respect, Boy, he of the foreign nickname, is as thoroughly English as he is Spanish.

The leavetaking scene at the end of the novel, where Paco and Boy see each other for the last time, is memorable. The reader experiences the truth of that saying "Partir c'est mourir un peu" (To say farewell is to die a little):

"Goodbye, Boy."
Goodbye, chico" he replied, stretching out his hand to me from the horse. And quickly rearing around, he continued on his way. . . . But he had scarcely gone six paces when he very rapidly turned around again. . . . He leaped from the horse, leaving it abandoned, and he charged toward me and embraced me, pushing his face close to mine. . . . I felt the wetness on my cheeks, and when Boy let me go his face was covered with tears. . . . Then, in a natural voice, but heartrending in its very naturalness, as the sorrow of strong men always is, he said to me: "There you go, lad, you must be very happy now! . . . You have seen me cry! . . . The glory is yours! . . . Now for sure we are 'Romeo and Juliet' "

A Paradox: Luis Coloma and Ramón del Valle-Inclán

Chapter 28 takes place in the midst of the Carlist civil war, where Boy is shot by the militia (*migueletes*). The page describing his interment is so unusual as to require commentary here. The *migueletes,* believing Boy to be a foreign citizen, are frightened and hastily bury him:

Soon the hole was dug, wide and fairly deep, and first taking the watch and money from the cadaver, they threw it into the pit. . . . But it turned out that the grave was too short, and the feet of the dead man, which were well tied together now, stuck out over the end by about two hand lengths. The young miguelete wanted to lengthen the grave, but the old man violently opposed this with a devilish look, and he struck three or four blows with the edge of his pick on the dead man's legs; the bones crunched horribly on being splintered, and now that they were flexible like a sheet of paper, he folded the legs upward, and as quickly as he could began to throw earth in the grave until it was filled. The young miguelete, as yellow as wax, turned his face away, horrified.

The *migueletes* leave, but one other person witnessed the burial, the Basque woman Juana-Mari, who was hidden behind a door: "She stuck her head out, trembling, livid with horror, her eyes still dilated by fright. . . ."

It is curious that this terrible scene resembles the creations of Spain's great modern satirist, Ramón del Valle-Inclán (1866–1936). No one could be further removed from Valle than the devout Paco Burunda or his author Luis Coloma, S. J. Valle's *Sonatas* make a mockery of traditional values, and his aesthetic primer, *The Marvelous Lamp,* carries a subtitle, *Spiritual Exercises,* that is a patent spoofing of St. Ignatius Loyola's famous work of the same title. Valle's exercises proclaim an aesthetic gnosis based on a mixture of ancient pantheistic and Gnostic, particularly Manichaean, elements. In one part of *The Marvelous Lamp* he declares that gnostics like himself take delight in creating the grotesque, which accounts for the weird, uncanny scenes in his literature. Valle has been accused of a lack of seriousness, an inaccurate charge because his outlandish scenes and jokes are never merely that; sometimes they satirize, sometimes they provide an unforgettable experience of an era or event, for example, the Carlist War, and at all times they offer an artistic delight, which Valle would claim to be a gnostic pleasure.

What, on the other hand, will account for the grotesque interment of Boy? It certainly does not consciously come from anything as heterodox as *The Marvelous Lamp* or its anti-Jesuitic, anti-Catholic author Valle-Inclán. Valle would have likened Coloma to the hypocritical clergy of the *Sonatas,* with their "ojos entornados" (half-closed eyes), and Coloma would certainly have grouped Valle with Renan, Frazer, "revolutionary traitors," and even worse, with demonic forces, given the sacrilegious scenes of Valle's works. The answer then must lie somewhere beyond the conscious, and there we may find two reasons. Coloma (1851–1916) and Valle-Inclán (1866–1936) were contemporaries, and they must have had similar experiences. Valle-Inclán's *The Marvelous Lamp* shows a formal Manichaean disdain of matter: the senses are evil and not to be trusted, and time, "the sterile Satan" as he calls it, is also evil. Valle does not like or place confidence in the world about him and seeks something outside it, the world of mystery, which can be captured somehow by the artist: "Listen to the music of my words, not to their meaning." Coloma, who believed in the Incarnation of Christ, could never disdain matter with the same intensity as Valle-Inclán, and he certainly could not call it inherently evil; nevertheless, there is in all his literature a certain antinomy between matter and spirit that has a nonorthodox savor. His otherworldliness seems excessive. Thus, both Coloma the Jesuit and Valle the anti-Jesuit may have had a common experience and sympathy; witnessing the last three decades of the nineteenth century, the Generation of Materialism as one historian has called it,[3] they may both have reacted by creating grotesque scenes in their literature. In Coloma's case, this might mean that the *migueletes* could mutilate the body of Boy because his shriven soul had already ascended to heaven.

The second similarity between Coloma and Valle-Inclán can be seen in the former's active contradiction of his own verbal profession. He professed to be a missionary-novelist whose pulpit (*cátedra*) was the novel, and, to be sure, he seems to play that role throughout his *Recreational Readings,* some passages of *Bagatelles,* and a few parts of *Boy.* But, as we have seen, he is sometimes carried away by his satirical muse and talent for storytelling: the novelist acquires the upper hand. He is good at aesthetic deformation and enjoys doing it, so he creates his Villamelones, Frasquitos, Diogenes, and the final scene of *Boy.* He may not subscribe to the aesthetic gnosis of Valle-Inclán with its anti-Christian musical score, but he does experience a peculiar delight, a *gnosis* of sorts, in creating his marionettes and belittling them, and thus he resembles Valle. His antimaterialism and the pleasure he takes in narration make him a cousin, albeit distant, of the goat-bearded, one-armed, turban-hatted sage of Galicia. The similarities I have suggested stop short at the threshold of prose style. Coloma condemns materialism harshly, in its own terms, *sans façon,* whereas Valle creates a superior music. Hence he calls his works *Sonatas.*

Chapter Five
Retratos de antaño and
El marqués de Mora

In addition to his stories and novels, Coloma wrote six biographies about historical figures such as Cardinal Cisneros, Mary Stuart, Don John of Austria, the Villahermosa family, and his own famous friend Fernán Caballero. He so embellished these biographies with imaginary dialogues and situations that they became novelistic histories rather than biography in the traditional sense of the genre. The present chapter will examine two of them, *Retratos de antaño* (Portraits of yore) and *El marqués de Mora* (The marquis de Mora); the remaining biographies will appear in chapters 6–7.

Portraits of Yore concerns three members of the Villahermosa family in the eighteenth century, namely, the saintly María Pignatelli, her husband the duke of Villahermosa, and their cousin, the marquis de Mora; *The Marquis de Mora,* as the title indicates, continues the history of one of them. Coloma wrote these books at the request of his friend, the duchess of Villahermosa, who kept pressing him to write, for she was anxious to perpetuate the memory of her saintly grandmother. Coloma, as it turned out, devoted most of his pages to the concupiscent marquis de Mora rather than María Pignatelli. Perhaps he unconsciously sensed the drama in Mora's short life and hopeless love with Mademoiselle de Lespinasse, for his pages on this black sheep of the Villahermosas are among the best he ever penned.

Portraits of Yore and *The Marquis de Mora* develop the same theme as *Bagatelles.* María Pignatelli, a girl of fourteen, marries the duke of Villahermosa and travels with him through Europe. She goes to England, meets Lord Chesterfield and Horace Walpole, attends the theater of the day, and witnesses the actions of "impious men" and frivolous women, although, according to Coloma, English customs were not as bad as those of Paris. Then María goes to the scandalous French court with the duke, where she makes the acquaintance of Marie Antoinette and other French ladies. She decides to remain secluded and to play

the role of the perfect wife (Fray Luis de León's *perfecta casada*), until
one day her confessor, an anonymous priest whom the court nicknames
Albertus Magnus, advises her that a virtuous woman can live in the
world and put up with vice without compromising with it.[1]

There are, however, other women at court who lose their virtue
through the bad example they see there—they are scandalized—and
still others, vain, frivolous women, who bring their daughters there to
show them off. Of the frivolous women, Coloma writes: "because it is
a constant phenomenon that ought to open the eyes of vain ladies who
place all their ambition in creating for themselves a vain renown; that
malicious gossip always punishes their foolishness, transforming their
superficialities into faults, their errors into sins, converting at times,
in the eyes of the populace and even of History herself, a woman who
is merely frivolous or imprudent into a Messalina or Cleopatra." This
is the style of the moralizer who composed most of the *Recreational
Readings* and intruded into some of the chapters of *Bagatelles.*

At least half of *Portraits of Yore* and all of its sequel, *The Marquis de
Mora,* have nothing to do with the saintly María Pignatelli or her husband the duke of Villahermosa and everything to do with that other
side of the family, the lustful and "impious" José Pignatelli y Gonzaga,
marquis de Mora, who was born in 1744 and died thirty years later of
tuberculosis. Mora had several friends among the French radicals, the
most prominent of whom was D'Alembert, leader of the *philosophes* and
editor of the *Encyclopédie.* By a strange alliance, Mora was not only the
good friend of D'Alembert, he was also the lover of the latter's mistress, Mademoiselle de Lespinasse.

Coloma edits and translates many letters that the great Frenchman
wrote to Mora and his family in Spain. D'Alembert is much concerned
about the health of the tubercular marquis and keeps arguing that he
should come to Paris, where the air is much better for the lungs. Since
he is writing at the behest of his mistress, he is cast in the role of a
tertiary, a *celestino* so to speak, who beseeches Mora to visit France
ostensibly for his health but really for the love of la Lespinasse.

The letters of D'Alembert have the importunate air of a woman
begging her lover to come join her, and it is said that at least one of
the letters, dated 14 March 1774 (see *OC,* 776) was really dictated to
him by Mademoiselle de Lespinasse. It seems strange that Coloma the
moralist, writing at the command of a duchess anxious to preserve the
memory of her saintly ancestor, is principally writing about a love affair
in which a famous *philosophe* begs a charming and handsome Spanish

nobleman to come visit his own mistress. And he writes about it effectively, for the French chapters and intercalated letters are some of the most memorable pages of the book. One is reminded of the prologue to the Arcipreste de Hita's fourteenth century *The Book of Good Love,* in which the great poet argued that in order to know good love one must also know foolish love and so he will put the two side by side, religious verses and seductive verses. One may argue whether or not the Arcipreste was talking with tongue in cheek, but no one can make such an argument concerning Coloma. It would seem that the artist in him instinctively knew that too much preaching would destroy the book, and so once again the novelist got the better of the missionary and had his way. Hallowed or not, the love of Mademoiselle de Lespinasse for Don José Pignatelli y Gonzaga, marquis de Mora, is truly unforgettable.

Since Coloma is acting as a historian in these biographies, it behooves us to say something about his historiography. First, as a Jesuit, he always writes *pro domo sua.* The books under study here include the count of Aranda and his expulsion of the Jesuits from Spain, in 1767, during the reign of Charles III. Coloma dislikes Aranda and the influence of the French *philosophes* and their Spanish friends on him. He speaks of "the venomous influence of that diabolical old man," Voltaire, and again excoriates the Masonic lodges. But he can see virtue in Charles III, who he says led a good personal life. He devotes a few pages to Charles's "routine life" and his love of the hunt; on the other hand, he does not write a single line about the economic questions confronting the monarchy. This was not rare in the nineteenth century, when many authors still wrote histories basically military and political in scope. As for Coloma himself, his historiographic credo can be reduced to one line, from chapter 1 of *The Marquis de Mora:* "because the cornerstone of every society has always been an altar stone, and when this stone is removed or tumbled down, the society is removed or tumbled down with it." Thus historical causation is reduced to a religious cornerstone.

The marquis de Mora may be lustful, but his actions are reprehensible for more transcendental reasons: he is impious, a man without faith, without religion, a man who prides himself on his friendship with French atheists, a man who tumbles altar stones. On the other hand, the duke of Villahermosa is also a rake in his youth, but he keeps the faith, and guided by the saintly example of his young wife he becomes truly a holy man in later life. Mora's French friends are not reproved primarily because they are out to strip the church of its wealth or because they yearn for political power, or even because they are lustful. After all, the duke of Villahermosa was lustful as a young man.[2] No, the *philosophes* were villains because they took away and tore down the cornerstone of society, the altar.

There are many memorable passages in these books on María and José Pignatelli. I particularly remember three of them. In chapter 6 of *Portraits of Yore* Coloma writes: "It has been said that the world is a comedy for the man who thinks and a tragedy for the man who feels; no comedy, really, more ridiculous for the intellect, no tragedy more sorrowful for the heart, than that played by French society in the latter half of the eighteenth century." This dichotomy provides a key to everything Coloma ever wrote, including his novel *Bagatelles*. As a thinking man he can look at the enemies of Spanish and French tradition with scorn, and if his satirical muse quickens him he can take a scalpel and ruthlessly expose the entrails of Spanish politicians and French paramours, making them ridiculous for the intellect. On the other hand, as a feeling man he can see those same politicians and paramours corrupt young people, depriving them of their virtue and their faith, and he can bleed internally before the tragedy; the remedy for the tragedy, to the extent that there is one, is preaching. Thus we have returned to the missionary-novelist or novelist-missionary. When a thoughtful Coloma writes about the passing scene he writes a satirical novel; and when a heartful Coloma writes about it he preaches within that novel. From these premises it would seem to follow that novelists *qua* novelists should think more than they feel. The feeling will give the impetus needed for writing, but this impetus must be given form by thought.

Another memorable passage is the following sentence from chapter 13, *Portraits of Yore*: "This was the life of the marquis de Mora on his return from France, as it was of many dandies (*petimetres*) of his era, in whom one can already see that strange mixture of foreignism and flashiness (*extranjerismo y majeza*) that still characterizes quite a few of the elegant people of our time." It is interesting that an author quite different from Coloma, the comediographer Jacinto Benavente (1866–1954), has made an observation about Restoration Spain in almost the same words:

In these years of the Restoration, the air, the tone of Madrilenian society lay between the Frenchy and the flashy (*era entre afrancesado y chulesco*). The return of aristocratic emigrés and of monarchists attached to the Bourbon dynasty brought fashions and customs from abroad, and at the same time Hispanism was carried to an extreme, with the desire of Hispanizing the restoration of the king in order to provide a contrast with the brief interregnum of a foreign king and of a republic badly copied from the French; this was especially so in everything difficult for foreigners to understand. So that between the bad copying of things from outside and the exaggeration of things from within, everything came to look foreign, and, to tell the truth, a caricature. Alfonso XII was always the gentleman Teddy Boy (*el señorito achulado*), as his son Alfonso XIII was always the foreignish young blade from Madrid.[3]

Coloma speaks of *petimetres, extranjerismo y majeza* among eighteenth-century Spaniards, and Benavente of *señorito achulado, afrancesado y chulesco* in nineteenth-century Madrid: the thought is the same.

A third passage is striking because of its love story and attention to detail. Coloma cites the will and testament of Mademoiselle de Lespinasse (*Portraits of Yore*, chapter 15):

I ask Monsieur D'Alembert, at the time of my death, to have the goodness to look in my pockets or my bureau drawer for two portraits of the deceased marquis de Mora; he will have to take from me a ring with a lock of hair in it that I have always worn on my finger; he will also have to take from my watch two little hearts that hang from the chain, one made of hair and the other of gold; he will put all this in a little box and he will send it to the duchess of Villahermosa with a letter making it clear that I am the one who saw to it on my death that the box was carefully sent to her. It would be advisable to entrust the count of Aranda with the sending of the box.

D'Alembert apparently carried out the will of his friend and sent everything to the duchess of Villahermosa. Coloma writes:

The portraits and the symbolical hearts have disappeared; the ring with the hair is on our desk at the present time, in the company of another ring given by Lespinasse to Mora. The first of these rings consists of a band of gold bound by a braid of dark blond hair, joined at both ends by a plate of gold with the letters: *Mémoire de. . . .* The second ring is formed by a band of gold with a perpetual monthly calendar sculpted on it and a plate on which there is a motto about the memory of a dead man that can't be read a century later without a certain fearful sorrow; *Que tout passe hors l'amour.*

Everything passes away except love. Coloma has recorded here an absorbing love story in the tradition of Tristan and Iseult.[4]

Some Letters of Coloma

Coloma wrote the two biographies just described at the request of the duchess of Villahermosa, who was María Pignatelli's granddaughter. Since he was constantly writing the duchess, one can trace the development of these books in a volume called *Epistolario del P. Luis Coloma, S. J.* (Letters of Father Luis Coloma, S. J.)

From the letters we learn that the first two chapters of *Portraits of Yore* were published in the *Sacred Heart Messenger* in November 1891 and then republished elsewhere. Coloma does not object to the republication as such, but complains about the numerous typographical errors, which detract from the story. He asks the duchess to send him the biography of a certain D. Ramón Pignatelli, mentions a marriage certificate of the marquis de Mora, and says he is trying to trace the diary of the monks of Veruela. He notes that no chapter was published in June 1891, but another one appears in the *Messenger* of July. He has the baptismal certificates of Mora and his son and is trying to ascertain whether the signature on a certain letter is Mora's. He knows the letters of Mademoiselle de Lespinasse "by heart," having read them so often. He learns that in Vienna they are translating his chapters into German as they appear, one by one. The duchess apparently keeps urging him to write, for he frequently alludes to his poor health and to certain bibliographical problems: can she move some of her papers and books to one of her estates near where he is residing? The chapter for December 1892 was sent to the printer's on time, but obstacles there will hold it up until the January 1893 issue of the *Messenger.* In the course of his studies he makes some important discoveries; for example, the more than forty volume diary of a certain Father Luengo, in which he learns that the count of Aranda, who was persecuting the Jesuits, had an illegitimate half-brother, a Jesuit, whom he protected in the midst of the persecution. These *Letters* to the duchess of Villahermosa continue until the end of 1892, and then there are a few more letters to her children, one of them as late as 1914. Among other things, they show how intimate Coloma was with members of the aristocracy.

Chapter Six
Three Histories
La reina mártir

The subtitle of *La reina mártir* (The martyr queen), a biography of Mary Queen of Scots, is *Historical Sketches of the Sixteenth Century,* the word *sketches* determining the structure of the book. Coloma is rather like an artist sketching the picture of various persons of the sixteenth century; Catherine de Medicis; her daughter-in-law, Mary Stuart; John Knox; James Stuart, Mary's bastard brother; Mary's second husband, Darnley; her third husband, Bothwell; George Douglas; Murray; the duke of Norfolk; Higford; Prince James, Gilbert Gifford; Tony Babington; Walsingham; two Jesuits; Elizabeth, queen of England; and Essex. The book takes sides, and in this sense is unlike one of its principal sources, François A. M. Mignet's *Histoire de Marie Stuart.* The Reformation and the heretical church of Elizabeth are as repulsive as the queen herself; John Knox is fanatical; Murray and Higford are traitors; Walsingham is infamous; and Gilbert Gifford is the Iscariot. This does not prevent the author from speaking dispassionately about some of the Protestants or from lamenting the massacre of the Huguenots on St. Bartholomew's Day. Here, as in Coloma's other histories, almost no attention is given to economic causes. All motivation is theological and religious, so that the characters become malevolent or virtuous, depending on the correctness of their position.

The nature of the sketches lends a novelistic style to the book. Chapters 16 and 17 of book 2, which employ the clock routine, will serve as a good example of how the episodes are written. On 25 April 1568 Mary Stuart had changed her dress for that of a washerwoman named Meg, had entered a rowboat, and almost effected an escape across Lake Lochleven near the castle of the Douglas family, when her two oarsmen became suspicious and returned her to her prison. Her followers agreed that should another escape ever be planned, someone would signal by thrice singing the first two verses of an ancient Douglas ballad. Then:

And it happened that, the queen one day doing needle-work with her ladies next to the window of the drawing room, they suddenly heard in the garden a delicate little child's voice that deliberately sang:

Oh Douglas, Douglas,
faithful and good!

The three women were surprised, pale, and frightened, looking at one another in the greatest silence. A bit later the little voice sounded again in the garden, with the same cadence and deliberateness:

Oh Douglas, Douglas,
faithful and good!

Then at a sign from the queen, Mary Seaton peeped out the window and saw Douglitas, the little page of Lady Douglas, seated solemnly on the ground near the foot of the tower, setting a bird trap with the greatest attention. At that moment Douglitas repeated again:

Oh Douglas, Douglas,
faithful and good!

Then the queen went down to the garden with Mary Seaton and Lady Fleming so as to meet the boy as if by chance; but he, now that the trap was set, withdrew with the greatest indifference, without seeming to even notice the presence of the ladies.

The above event happened in April and nothing seemed to come of it when in May they again heard the voice of Douglitas, who was writing letters in the sand and erasing them as he wrote them: "Be ready to-night at nine. Don't open unless they give you the password from outside." Then he walked away from the bird trap, singing: "Oh Douglas, Douglas, / faithful and good!" The ladies debate the reliability of such a puny messenger, but at nightfall the bonfires begin to glow on Kinross hill and the mountain opposite, a signal that help was at hand. After curfew, the ladies make their preparation and wait. "It must have been about eight thirty," . . . but they "did not quite understand how Douglitas could tear the keys away from the dangerous claws" of the chatelaine.

The next chapter (17) describes the stratagem of Douglitas, George

Douglas, and Beton, and the successful flight of Mary Stuart at nine o'clock. It is a well-paced escape scene, ending with the interesting observation: "Two hundred and fifty years later, in 1818, a fisherman from Kinross taking out his nets one day found hooked in the rig those historical keys of Lochleven castle that Douglitas had thrown to the bottom of the lake the memorable night of the queen's flight." This episode marks the end of book 1, just prior to Mary Stuart's journey to England, where she planned to take refuge. It makes a fitting contrast to book 2, "The Aunt and the Niece" (that is, Elizabeth and Mary), which tells the story of Mary's nineteen-year imprisonment in England, before her death by execution. Book 1 ends with excitement, whereas book 2 begins tranquilly with an uncomprehending niece seeking aid from her kin.

Once again in *The Martyr Queen* the reader can see Coloma's predilection for the French language and culture. Speaking of Mary's youth in France, he describes the death of Francis II and the reactions of his mother, Catherine de Medicis, and of his wife, the nineteen-year-old Mary Stuart. The latter is thoroughly French, and when her mother-in-law succeeds in sending her to Scotland, she writes her own verses:

> Adieu plaisant pays de France!
>   O ma patrie
>   La plus chérie,
> qu'as nourri ma jeune enfance.
> Adieu France! Adieu nos beaux jours!
>   La nef qui dejoint nos amours
> n'a eu de moi que la moitié:
> Une partie te reste, elle est tienne:
> Je la fie a ton amitié,
>   pour que de l'autre il te souvienne.

> Farewell fair land of France!
>   Oh my country
>   The dearest,
> you who have harbored my youth
> Farewell France! Farewell our glorious days!
>   The ship that separates our love
> has only the half of me:
> A part remains, it is yours:

I entrust it to your friendship
to remind you of the other half of me.

Mary Stuart usually wrote her letters in French, and throughout the book Coloma quotes them in Spanish, putting the French original in a footnote. In the last chapter, just before Mary's execution, he imagines the following words, directed to her steward, Andrew Melvil: "Don't cry, my good Melvil; rather be glad, because Mary Stuart has come to the end of her misfortunes. . . . You know full well that this world is nothing but vanity, disorder, and misery. . . . Tell the whole world that I die firm in my religion; a true Catholic, a true Scot, and a true French lady. May God pardon those who desire my death, and he, who sees the secret thoughts of men, knows that I have always desired the union of Scotland and England." Coloma was naturally attracted to the sixteenth century and to a queen like Mary Stuart, who suffered martyrdom for her faith. One suspects he was also attracted to her because she spoke and wrote in a language dear to his heart.

Coloma's historical bias is reflected in his prose. When writing about Higford, the secretary who betrayed the duke of Norfolk, he mentions "a black treason" and "this miserable man." When speaking of Mary's opponents he also resorts to zoological imagery, sometimes mixing his metaphors; thus he writes of Queen Elizabeth: "Finally Elizabeth herself realized it, and then she made one of her snake twists. . . . She gave Paulet the order to play deaf and dumb in everything concerning Mary's correspondence, without relaxing his surveillance of her, and even to provide her occasions when she might send out her mail. Once the poor fly was given room to soar, the spider lay in ambush in her lair and spread out her repugnant web" (book 2, chapter 9). At times the style is sententious. Amyas Paulet, mentioned above, survived four different reigns in which there were many political and religious persecutions. When asked how he managed to do so, he replied: "Being a willow and not an oak."

Coloma did not employ as many primary sources for *The Martyr Queen* as he did for *Portraits of Yore* and *The Marquis de Mora*. He mentions several secondary authorities he relied on, the most prominent of which are Pedro de Ribadeneyra's *Ecclesiastical History of the Schism of the Kingdom of England* (1588) and François A. M. Mignet's *Histoire de Marie Stuart* (1851). Ribadeneyra, one of the first Jesuits, based his history on the writings of others and on his experiences in England during the reign of Mary Tudor.

Jeromín

In a letter dated 12 April 1903, the eminent novelist Emilia Pardo Bazán wrote the following passage to Coloma:

My dear and respected friend: This is the second letter I am writing you to thank you for sending me the interesting book about Don John of Austria. The first was lost in the street. . . . The lost letter said no more than what this one will say: that the book is delightful for its pleasantness and narrative liveliness, and also that it is written without the desire of vindicating Philip II in everything and for everything, an undertaking more difficult than laudable in which other Catholic authors have gotten bogged down by confusing Christian apologetics with monarchical apologetics. Without overstating things or making Philip II a monster and a parricide, which indeed he wasn't, you recognize several of his errors, and above all his gravest error of distrust and suspicion against Don John (who was worth a hundred times more than he). Weakness of character, the principal defect of Philip II, was what put him at the mercy of the intriguer, Antonio Pérez. You make this obvious.[1]

Jeromín (the nickname of Don John of Austria, whose baptismal name was Jerome) tells the story of this well-loved hero's youth, of the battle of Lepanto, and of Philip II's attempts to limit his activity. The king was extremely jealous of his illegitimate half-brother's fame, and were it not for his opposition, Don John might have founded a lasting kingdom in Africa.

The structure of Jeromín, whose subtitle is Historical Studies of the Sixteenth Century, resembles that of The Martyr Queen: Historical Sketches of the Sixteenth Century; the mode is episodic, permitting the author to examine whatever he desires: a legend, the alleged heresy of Archbishop Carranza, the death of Charles V at Yuste, an auto da fe, the perverse sickness of the prince Don Carlos, the rebellion of Aben-Humeya, the Battle of Lepanto, the question of Antonio Pérez, the attempts against Escovedo's life, and other events of Spanish history. The connecting thread throughout the book is the character and presence of Don John of Austria. Without explicitly using the term "hero in history," Coloma indicates that this concept is the basis of his historiography; in the epitaph to book 1, chapter 1, he writes: "Fuit homo missus a Deo, cui nomen est Ioannes" (There was a man sent by God, whose name was John—John 1:6). Thus the Battle of Lepanto was not a happenstance or the result of economic or political causes but a special act within the divine plan.

Coloma wrote a preface to *Jeromín* ("To the Reader," 24 January 1903) that explains his intentions in writing his biographies. He says he does not propose to disentangle the profound problems of history nor to unearth previously unknown documents. He proposes rather to "popularize" (the italics are Coloma's)[2] some figures connected with transcendental events of history and to examine them in the light of reason and Catholic criteriology. Therefore, he has not read everything he could on the subject; he has accepted what is certain and chosen what seems most likely from doubtful evidence; and he has "tried later with his imagination and the study of the era to revive those dead people and to give life, relief, and a contemporary atmosphere to the whole ensemble." Thus Coloma will employ the novelist's art to vivify a historical figure or event, in order to popularize it.

This reader was struck by two aspects of *Jeromín*; first, by the similarities between the book and Cervantes's *Exemplary Tales*. The young Don John, Jeromín, resembles Don Juan de Cárcamo in *The Little Gypsy Girl*, or Preciosa in the same story, or Costanza in *The Illustrious Kitchen Maid*, or the young boys in *Rinconete and Cortadillo*. His birth is shrouded in mystery, and there is constant mention of a "mysterious correspondent" interested in him, who turns out to be no one less than Philip II, king of Spain. Philip finally tells him they are brothers, and then, at the age of eighteen, Don John sets out for Barcelona without permission to fight against the Turk; he even confronts an evil opponent (like Juana Carducha of *The Little Gypsy Girl*) in the person of the prince Don Carlos, who apparently committed a perverse act in his presence:

Don Carlos ordered the doors to be shut and no one has found out exactly what went on between uncle and nephew during the two hours they remained within. At the end of that time the chamber aides heard a clamor inside and the vigorous and manly voice of Don John of Austria, who was angrily shouting: *Hold on, Your Majesty!* Frightened, they opened the door and Don John appeared flashing fire from his eyes, holding at bay with his sword the Prince, who with another sword and a dagger, livid with rage, was trying to attack him.

The unusual events of *Jeromín* suggest either that the plots of Cervantes's tales may be less fantastic than they appear to be, or that Coloma's vision of a Golden Age hero is Cervantine: like Cervantes's Preciosa, the little gypsy, Don John had nobility of blood (*nobleza de sangre*), and so he could perform unusual feats.

The second striking feature of the book is the stable character of Don John, who appears as a tower of strength among so many lesser men: "He conquered with clemency, he governed benignly. . . . he knew how to choose his advantages, he measured his forces, he affably appeared before his soldiers and he commanded them in a pleasant way. Because of this and because he spoke to everyone in their mother tongue, he held so many different kinds of people in obedience."[3]

Fray Francisco

Four figures stand out among Luis Coloma's historical heroes: Ferdinand III (1201–52), the canonized saint who united the kingdoms of Castile and Leon; Isabel the Catholic (1451–1504), whose reign saw the union of Castile and Aragon; Cardinal Cisneros (1436–1517), Isabel's able chancellor, who laid the foundation of the modern Spanish state; and Don John of Austria (1545–78), who destroyed the Moslem fleet at Lepanto. Two of these figures, Isabel and her chancellor, are studied in *Fray Francisco,* the biography of Gonzalo Jiménez de Cisneros, who took the name *Fray Francisco* on entering the Franciscan order.

The book begins with the year 1465, a time of "treachery, perfidy and surprise." Even the archbishop of Toledo, primate of Spain, Don Alonso Carrillo, was waging war with his fellow feudal lords against the crown. The monarchy had fallen to such a depth that Carrillo and other nobles had a clay statue made of the king, whom they abused in effigy on a public scaffold. The deed was so horrible that some of the nobles and people reacted, favoring the king, and had a similar statue made of their archbishop. They called it "Don Opas," after a legendary traitor of early Spanish history. The whole kingdom was up in arms. What would be the result? Here Coloma answers with the providential hero: "When providence has some plan, it is scarcely important to it what instruments and what means it makes use of. In its hands everything is thunder, everything is tempest, everything is deluge, everything is Alexander or Caesar" (*OC,* 1472). These words, which Coloma quotes from the French of Balzac, attribute to providence a peculiar nonchalance that may also be found in providence's surrogates, Queen

Isabel, Cardinal Cisneros, . . . and Luis Coloma. The events of the years encompassed by the book, 1465–95, are fascinating, and Coloma presents them as his Providence might, as deluge, as thunder. The characters opposing these forces must necessarily be overcome.

At times the narrator, Coloma, reveals himself as the *laudator temporis acti*. Of the events preceding the wedding of Isabel and Don Fernando de Aragón, he writes: "and deliberately and majestically there appeared on the plain the two retinues of the king and the princess, walking slowly until they met in front of the Inn, without anybody suspecting perhaps that from that meeting there was to blossom, after a brief and cruel struggle, the colossal and glorious Spain of the future of that era, which today is no more than a memory . . ." (*OC*, 1486). Coloma's attitude toward Spain is just the opposite of that of the Generation of 1898. He praises the ancient *casticismo* (Spanish essence) of God, king, and country, whereas the intellectuals who followed him came to question it and even scorn it.

At times Coloma will introduce some extraneous or anachronistic material into his narrative that is refreshing. Of the adulterous wife of Henry IV, mother of Juana la Beltraneja, he writes: "Five centuries before the invention of automobiles and before the ladies of today had thought up the helpful *cachepoussière* (dust shield), this coquette of the fifteenth century had already known how to use her wits so as to arrive without the slightest rumple, after a journey of two leagues on horseback along the roads of that era" (*OC*, 1507). This sort of wry remark may be what Coloma himself referred to as Andalusian humor. In *Fray Francisco*, a pious woman Mari López is called Mari-Cuervo (Mary-Crow) because "the Andalusians of that time must have been as merry and fond of making fun and jokes as they are right now . . ." (*OC*, 1527).

In one footnote Coloma introduces the Revolution of 1868, which was ever present in his mind, into this history of the fifteenth century. Speaking of Cisneros's reform of the secular and regular clergy, he says that Queen Isabel visited a convent in Seville called Mother of God, where the nuns were edified by her piety. Then he writes:

The impious fury of the Revolution of September 1868 expelled these exemplary religious women from their convent of the Mother of God, and tore the modest edifice to the ground, tearing down at the same time what they used to call *The little house of the Queen,* which were the rooms that Isabel the Catholic occupied during that Lenten season, and which the nuns had kept intact until that time with great veneration. The person who writes these lines had the opportunity of seeing the rich and curious Moorish tiles that used to adorn the above-said rooms. The ignorant and rapacious revolutionaries sold them outside of Spain at a very high price. (*OC,* 1530)

Coloma did not live to finish his study of Cardinal Cisneros, which takes the reader down to 1495, the year Fray Francisco was installed as archbishop of Toledo. An Argentine Jesuit, Alberto Risco, finished the story of Cisneros in a second volume.

Chapter Seven
Recuerdos de Fernán Caballero
A Sentimental Journey

In the *Recuerdos de Fernán Caballero* (Memories of Fernan Caballero) Coloma writes a meandering encomium of his dear friend of yesteryear, who was fifty-five years his senior. He must have had a filial love for her since he refers to her "maternal laugh" and "maternal tenderness." This gentle lady from Andalusia occupied a prominent place in his thoughts, and now he, sixty years of age and broken in health, was going to pay her one last tribute.

He recalls many events of Caballero's life: a painting of her by Federico Madrazo, the conversion of her famous father to Catholicism, her long residence in Germany, the battle of Trafalgar which she witnessed when she was nine years old, the French at Cádiz, her three marriages (two of them unhappy), her writing to Washington Irving, her generosity and subsequent poverty; but above all he recalls her as a gentle, kindly woman from the Andalusia of olden days when people were somehow better, a woman to whom he could write the following words on his entrance into the seminary:

Goodbye, my old friend. It is probable we won't see each other again in this life, but we will see each other in the next, where you will not be Fernán the admirable but Fernán the good, and where we will speak of a celestial literature, which will have the angels as critics. I ask you for your blessing as I have asked my mother for hers, and as I sent her an embrace, so shall I send you one, tomorrow, when I pass through Seville on my way to France. (*OC*, 1469)

Coloma's *Memories of Fernán Caballero* are not a history, to be judged by the canons of that discipline, but a series of evocations, a sentimental journey, like the kiss he blew to "Fernán the good" from the train window as he passed through Seville.

Formulaic Phrases and Confidence

The narrator, Coloma, keeps reminding us with certain formulaic
phrases that he is writing from memory: "I heard Fernán Caballero
relate this dreadful episode a thousand times, which she herself kept a
very vivid memory of through her mother's accounts of it. . . ." Thus
begins the description of the pursuit of Captain General Francisco
María Solano, Marquis of Solano, by a lunatic mob (chapter 10): "A
thousand times I heard Fernán Caballero describe the luxury of the
opulent dwelling place of Don Pedro Strange, and especially the room
of Doña María Tucker, in which the outcome of the terrifying drama
took place. . . ." In María Tucker's room there was a sort of priest's
hole in which Solano hid before he was shot by a close friend, who
wanted to prevent his being hanged by the mob (chapter 11). The
narrator writes with a heroic memory, conscious that he is narrating a
saga of great deeds and events. He is not unlike a composer of medieval
epic poetry.

Similar formulaic phrases are employed in other chapters. In describing the death of Fernán Caballero's first husband, a ne'er-do-well, the
narrator confidently writes: "I am perfectly familiar with it, because I
heard it from the mouth of Fernán, and I can transcribe it with complete precision . . ." (chapter 18). Ordinary biographers cannot write
with the unwavering confidence of this narrator, because they do not
write about a deceased heroine and beloved friend who told the narrator
exactly what to say, or sing.

On another occasion (chapter 20), at a large gathering, Fernán Caballero received a message from a young relative whose life was in
danger. The narrator writes:

Cecilia [Fernán] took it not without wonderment and beneath the weight of
all those dangerous looks she read the following lines, which I cannot copy,
naturally, but whose substance and the major part of whose sentences I con-
serve among my notes just as I heard them from Fernán Caballero: "Dear
Cousin: Don't be surprised on reading this note nor make any movement that
will betray you in front of those barbarous reactionaries who surely must be
surrounding you. I have fled from the ship they were taking me a prisoner in
to Seville. . . ."

The note continues and closes with a humorous postscript. Once again
the words suggest a narrator with a peculiarly infallible memory, for

after all the notes are "just as I heard them from Fernán Caballero." And who but such a narrator could remember a postscript, forty years after the story was told and ninety years after the event took place? This narrator, moreover, is a skillful rhetorician, for in spite of his disclaimer he does copy the message—naturally.

The empirical phrases described above, and others—"Fernán told me . . ." (chapter 27) "I heard her say it many many times . . ." (chapter 28); "A curious anecdote she told me. . . ." (chapter 24); "I remember the scene of the two of us on a certain afternoon in April, in the huge living room of our house. . . ." (chapter 30)—these phrases inspire confidence in the reader and give the book an informal, chatty air, as if the narrator were thinking out loud.

Anecdotes

Coloma's *Memories of Fernán Caballero* are based on a series of anecdotes according to which this modest old lady led an adventurous life. When she was nine years old she and her neighbors witnessed the Battle of Trafalgar, from her own house and with an eyeglass: "the tender Cecilia received a terrifying impression, which lasted her all her life, and which she never remembered without feeling profoundly affected; it later provided her material for a sensitive little article which, with the title of *A Mother,* has been printed among her other works . . ." (chapter 6). The narrator's story of the young Cecilia and Trafalgar resembles a scene from Edgar Allan Poe or Gustavo Adolfo Bécquer. A neighboring lady, a general's wife, had three sons go off to fight at Trafalgar, and for six hours she and Cecilia's family had to listen to the cannon fire and watch the destruction with their eyeglass. Many mariners would not return. The general's wife beseeched the mercy of God, and finally the sons returned, one by one, at well paced intervals, in descending order of age. Just before the youngest son's return, she cried: "Tell me the terrible truth! Where is he? Where is my Manuel?" The young boy appears abruptly, and then:

Then the eyes of the mother are dry: happiness does not shine in them, nor does sorrow cloud them. Her countenance, a short while before so expressive with various emotions, is calm, like the sea the north has frozen. Her eyes look indifferently on the sons who surround her; her inert arms fall from their embrace; her face, a moving reflection of her vehement feelings, becomes cold and stupid.

"Oh, my God, my God!," The eldest of her sons exclaims terrified. "How imprudent we were! A belated sorrow! That mother's heart, so tender and long-suffering, could not stand so much felicity! She had lost her reason!"

One anecdote contains a humorous scene recalling the jokes the narrator played on Villemeloncito, Tío Frasquito and the other characters of *Bagatelles*.[1] Fernán Caballero's young cousin Leopold, an extreme liberal in spite of his social class, must seek refuge in Fernán's house when the duke of Angoulême invades Spain with "the hundred thousand sons of St. Louis." There is a price on his head. High spirited and roguish, he enamors a squint-eyed portly woman seventeen years his senior, the daughter of the judge who will try his case. Suddenly Leopold begins to squint, and when his beloved asks him why, he tells her that his ailment began the very first moment he saw her, and that was:

without doubt owing to the repercussion of her eyes on his own, of her dominating force and of the truth of the refrain which said, in Andalusia and beyond, that a person is left squint-eyed when he is charmed or subjugated by a wonderful spectacle or marvelous beauty; amorous phenomena never hitherto seen, which, however, the judge's daughter readily believed, for a reason similar without doubt to the one that inspired this couplet:

> Well focused sight
> doth penetrate,
> a young girl said
> whose sight was not straight.
> (*OC*, 1415)

Leopold decides to terminate his joke:

He fell asleep at last, or he pretended that he was sleeping, until at nightfall he woke up, asking the maid for a purgative, which he himself wrote the prescription for indicating also the dosage. They were some gray powders, and since the dosage was undoubtedly exaggerated, the maid said to him when she delivered them:
"The apothecary says it's for a horse."
"No, woman, for a filly mule (*mula*)," Leopold answered in bad humor. (*OC*, 1416)

Leopold stops squinting, goes to his beloved's house, and tells her that a gypsy of Triana cured him with some gray powders, and that he has brought her some so that she too can be cured. The girl takes the medicine, and the results are described by one of her servants to Leopold's maid. A story such as this may be of questionable taste, and it may or may not make entertaining reading, but it comes from Coloma's imagination rather than his memories. Some of the many other stories interspersed throughout the *Memories of Fernán Caballero* concern the famous bandit Diego de Corriente; four young men and a miraculous event; Fernán and the young Coloma in an intrigue involving the vacant throne of 1868 and the duke of Montpensier;[2] Fernán's novel *La familia de Alvareda*; the invasion of Cádiz; the duke of Wellington and food allegedly poisoned at a ball; Fernán's brutal first husband; her kindly second husband; her suicidal third husband; the history of Coloma's first literary effort; and Fernán Caballero's own unpublished work, *Mr. John Bell*. These stories are all mixed in with biography, history, fiction, couplets, and aphorisms, which make the *Memories of Fernán Caballero* a curious literary collection. Here as in other works of Luis Coloma there is a decided preference for the aristocracy (see chapter 33), a reverence for Andalusia and its sense of humor, and an amused attitude toward phlegmatic Englishmen and stolid Germans. The narrator of *Memories* prefers meridional ways to the cold septentrional culture of Angles and Saxons.

The *Memories* and Recent Criticism

When Coloma published the *Memories of Fernán Caballero* in 1907–10, his book was considered a primary source for many episodes in his deceased friend's life, especially for the years prior to 1857, about which very little was known.[3] Several biographers relied on Coloma for information concerning Fernán, for example, the story behind her portrait by Federico Madrazo, the conversion of her German Protestant father, a ball she attended in honor of the duke of Wellington, an episode involving Washington Irving, and a stay in Paris with Madame Recamier. Recent scholarship has shown that many of the events described by Coloma never really happened, or, if they did happen, not in the same way. One scholar speaks of "inexactitudes, mistaken dates, plagiaries," of "interesting legends invented by Coloma," of "novelistic fiction," of "pure invention," and of "a false story" in the *Memories of Fernán Caballero;* and he concludes that "that source which had always been considered the richest source for biographical information concerning Cecilia Böhl de Faber, the *Memories of Fernán Caballero* by Luis Coloma, is entirely lacking in historical value."[4]

Perhaps the terms "interesting legends," "pure invention," and "a false story" will allow the following interpretation: Coloma, who as a young man idolized Fernán Caballero, will improve many of the actions of his dear friend in order to dramatize them for the reader. He is like an old soldier recounting the battles of fifty years ago. Consequently his *Memories* should be examined not so much from the viewpoint of historiography as from the viewpoint of the novel, in which one expects to find embellished truth and a well-told story.

Chapter Eight
Three Other Writings

The *Spiritual Exercises*

Alfonso XIII, a posthumous son, was declared king at his birth on 17 May 1886. He began to rule in his own right on his sixteenth birthday, in 1902, and for this occasion Coloma wrote a series of six meditations called the *Spiritual Exercises*. A succinct statement of their author's religious, political, and social beliefs, they also display his narrative art. Coloma demonstrates his arguments with aphorisms and stories.

In the preamble the manner is ordinary: "I should begin by telling your majesty that I am not going to lay before you profound problems requiring an intellectual effort for their disentanglement . . . ; nor marvelous truths, which are only within the reach of wise men or extraordinary talents. . . . Far from that, the truths your majesty is going to consider here are current truths, popular ones, known to all . . . ; truths so often handled and well-known that they can be included in the category of truths of the famous John Bull,[1] who used to call a closed hand a fist. . . ." Coloma then relates the story of the epitaph on a usurer's gravestone: "Here lies the soul of Attorney Astudillo." Several students out on a spree came across the stone, did not know what to make of it, and went on their way, but one of them, reasoning that the grave contained a mystery, dug beneath the stone and discovered a leather bag with ten thousand ducats and a sheepskin inside. On the latter he read these words: "I declare you to be my heir, whoever you may be, for you have had the wit to discern the true meaning of the inscription; but I charge you to use the money better than I did." In the six meditations that follow Coloma reaches beneath Astudillo's stone to show King Alfonso some other important truths.

Meditations 1–3 are a study in finality and eschatology. God created man to love him and serve him in this world and to be happy with him in the next; he created the things of this world for the use of man; and he created the king as a vicarious father to care for his human family. In one striking line Coloma defines the material and spiritual as *Bread and Catechism:* a well-ordered society demands the proper distribution of both, and a king must labor toward this end. In the first meditation Coloma, expounding the meaning of eternity for those condemned to hell, wrote the most Jansenistic lines of all his literature:

To lose the soul is to lose God and to fall into the most horrible misfortune for all eternity . . . and does your majesty know what eternity is? . . . Neither does your majesty know it, nor do I; nor can anyone fathom entirely this awful idea. . . . One can, however, gather some idea of it through some examples and comparison. . . . Does your majesty remember the beach of San Sebastián? . . . Does he remember that sand semicircle that is left uncovered in the Cove when the tide is out? . . . Could the little grains of sand there on that beach be counted? . . . Impossible. . . . Well then: let your majesty suppose that a poor little ant takes a little grain of sand on that beach, and walking, walking at his own pace, he brings it to Madrid and he deposits it in Retiro Park. . . . And he returns once again to the beach, and he takes another little grain and he brings it to Madrid. . . . And he returns again, and he comes again. . . . How many years would that poor little ant need to bring by itself the entire beach of San Sebastián to Retiro Park in Madrid? . . . I will not say hundreds of years, but thousands on thousands of centuries would not be enough. . . . Would the years be so many, so many, that when the little ant finally finished its work eternity would also have finished? . . . No, when the little ant finished its work, it could not be said that eternity had yet begun; because eternity never ends, and that immense passage of time doesn't take away from it even a single second. . . . Then imagine something more: imagine that when the little ant begins its journey from San Sebastián to Madrid, Your Majesty begins to suffer a headache or toothache. . . . Imagine that at the same time your majesty's mother is taken away, the person you love the most, and that with this ache in the body and this anguish in the soul, your majesty begins to contemplate, alone and without help, the trips of the little ant, hoping that when it finishes its tasks your majesty will see your mother again and will stop suffering. . . . And when it finishes its task they say to you that it has to transport also the beach of Zarauz, and later the beach of Guetaria, and later that of Zumaya, and after that the entire world to another hemisphere. . . . And not even then have you done more than to begin to suffer. . . . Is it possible to think of a greater despair? Is it possible to think of a more profound horror? . . . Well, your majesty is a mathematician, raise it all to an infinite power, and the infinite horror that results, that . . . that is what it means to lose one's soul.

This passage will recall the Pascalian wager and the sermon of James Joyce in *A Portrait of the Artist as a Young Man.* Life is a game where the odds are fearsome, and everyone, even the king, Alfonso, must live it as if he were a taut bow. In the fourth meditation, the *Spiritual Exercises for the King Don Alfonso XIII* provide for wholesome games and recreation, because "Arco siempre armado, o flojo o quebrado" (The always drawn bow, either lax or broken), but the arguments there are less convincing than the little ant with his little grain of sand making his infinite rounds. One suspects that Luis Coloma himself was extremely taut, except perhaps at intervals, when he was carried away by grotesque creations like Villamelón, he of the full dentures at birth, and Tío Frasquito, he of the prosthetic cork buttocks. Art, as well as the sacraments, has some saving grace.

Not all of the *Spiritual Exercises* display the grimness of the little ant's impossible chores in the face of eternity. There are some humorous passages, and meditations 3 and 4 resemble Louis XIV's *Memoirs on the Art of Government,* which the French king wrote for the Dauphin should the latter succeed him at a young age. There is some good advice on leadership, on the king's selection of friends, and on his conduct toward politicians and courtesans: "Affability for all; confidence in a very few; familiarity with no one."[2] In keeping with his other books, Coloma omits economic considerations.

The History of the Relics of St. Francis Borgia

On 30 July 1901 the relics of St. Francis Borgia were moved to their final resting place in the church named for him on Flor Baja Street, Madrid. A stone was placed above the relics, with the inscription: "In this urn are deposited the remains of St. Francis Borgia, Fourth duke of Gandía and third general provost of the company of Jesus. The most noble house of the dukes of Medinaceli is perpetually the patron of these remains and to it belongs the right of caring for them whenever the fathers of the company cannot do so in their own church." Although the inscription contains no intentional irony, that *whenever,* rendered in the Spanish by the subjunctive mood ("Cuando Los Padres De La Misma Compañía No Puedan Hacerlo"), has a nuance that can only cause the reader, Jesuit or anti-Jesuit, to smile. The subjunctive seems to say: Here we go again![3]

The bones of St. Francis experienced an unusual peregrination, which is the subject of Coloma's *History.* They were moved from Rome to Madrid in 1617, and within this capital city from one church to another. When Charles III expelled the Jesuits in 1767 they came under the charge of the Oratory, and during the Napoleonic invasion (1808) they were threatened because of their valuable silver urn and also the general suppression of religious orders. The Oratory managed to escape the "Slaughter of the Friars" in 1835, but their church where the relics were housed was the first to be torn down. The duke of Medinaceli managed to save the urn with the relics of his saintly ancestor, after which their history was comparatively tranquil until 1901.

Coloma's *History of the Relics* offers the reader a thumbnail sketch of Spanish history from the duke of Lerma (1553–1625) to the Revolution of 1868 and a few events beyond. He has some interesting stories to tell, for example, that of the duchess who had the silver urn bronzed so that the French would not steal it. He describes the triumphal march celebrating St. Francis's canonization in 1671, the ceremonial coach, the pageantry of the fiestas, the literary competitions, the floats and decorations, but although he is pleased by the honor bestowed on his fellow Jesuit, he cannot help commenting, several times, on the "bad taste" of that "strange epoch," and once he speaks of the "sumptuous Churrigueresque contraption of the time." Coloma is logical and rationalist in taste. He likes well-defined laws, premises, an orderly unfolding of the laws, and clear-cut conclusions. He also displays a nineteenth-century bias, a positivistic zeal, for example, in his statistics of chapter II (*OC,* 979).

The Academy Speech: The Author of *Fray Gerundio,* Padre José Francisco de Isla (1706–81)

Coloma was nominated for a chair in the Royal Academy of Language on 2 January 1908, and he presented his acceptance speech, the only other formal requirement for admission, on 6 December of the same year. Owing to his ill health, the speech was read by the Marquis de Pidal.

The academy speeches of the day generally fell into three parts. First, an assertion of humility and gratitude, by which the author referred to his own scant merits and thanked the academy for overlooking them and admitting him. Second, a tribute to the deceased member, whose chair the reader of the speech was to occupy. And third, the main topic of the speech, the original subject the new academician had chosen to talk about.

He addresses himself to part 1 of his speech humorously, arguing that it is difficult to speak both well of oneself and ill of oneself. How can he say, like a certain Oriental poet: "I am not a rose, but I have lived next to one"? Finally, he imagines a conversation in which a friend tells him that the academicians have chosen him because they are wise, talented, and renowned. He is about to swell with pride, when his friend reminds him that the difference between fools and wise men is this: the former *say* foolish things whereas wise men *do* them.

Having wittily declared his humility he praises the memory of Valentín Gómez, the former occupant of his chair. The praise comes easily, for during the *Bagatelles* affair Gómez, a conservative Catholic, had defended him. This gives Coloma a chance to write a long paragraph on *Bagatelles*, which he insists was not a *novela de clave:*

then I wrote a series of short little novels, all of them inspired by times past. . . . I threw these creatures to the public, as a blind man might throw stones into a pool, without calculating the aim or being aware of the result. But one of them, longer than the others, and with the name of *Bagatelles,* made such an explosion, that it caused the same effect in my spirit as the first cold bath I took when I was a child—a mixture of surprise, fright, and the physical need of running. . . . I recall it very well. I entered the shower and with the greatest innocence I pulled the cord, as they had told me. . . . I pulled the cord innocently and right then there fell on me a shower, not of frozen pin pricks but of poisonous darts in the form of letters, pamphlets and articles in newspapers and magazines, which made me take refuge in my almost wild forests of Deusto, crying out: Oh unhappy one!

Coloma goes on to defend *Bagatelles,* declaring that it was never meant to be a libel.

The third part of Coloma's speech narrates in some seven thousand words the major episodes of Father Isla's life (1706–81). Coloma is obviously pleased with Isla's jestful, satirical manner in the face of foolish humanity: "and therefore P. Isla said with assurance, in that most witty as well as profound letter, that he had chosen from that time on to laugh at humanity instead of getting mad at it." Coloma recalls a delightful couplet inserted in Isla's novel, *Fray Gerundio:* "Yo conocí en Madrid una condesa / que apprendió a estornudar a la francesa" (I knew in Madrid a countess / Who learned to sneeze in French). Coloma admires *Fray Gerundio,* the satire that so effectively ridiculed the abuses of sacred oratory in eighteenth-century Spain that *Friar Gerund* has become a household word for bombastic preachers.

But above all Coloma admires Isla's courage, sanctity, and devotion

to the Jesuit order, which was expelled from Spain and all its posses-
sions in 1767. After 1758, the year *Fray Gerundio* was published, the
Inquisition suppressed his book, and after 1767 he lived for fourteen
years an exile, although Charles III gave him the option of remaining
in Spain. Isla stood by his brothers, one of whom was, at least poten-
tially, Luis Coloma.

There is a clue in Coloma's speech as to why he chose Padre Isla for
his topic. He says he had thought of discussing an ancestor, Carlos
Coloma (1573–1637), whose *Wars of the Netherlands* is considered a
classic of Golden Age prose; but it so happened that seventeen years
before his academy election, Valentín Gómez, the very man whose seat
he was taking in the academy, had written him an unforgettable letter.
Coloma had been accused of libeling certain persons in *Bagatelles:*

And see, gentlemen academicians, how events combined themselves, in such
a singular and unexpected manner. . . . Perplexed on seeing such a forceful
pen come to my defense, I hastened to write to Don Valentín Gómez, express-
ing my gratitude; and he, as kindly and considerate then as he had been
generous and noble previously, answered me with a letter in which he did not
even remotely suspect that I would one day succeed him in the academy. In
this letter I have found, after seventeen years, the theme of the speech I must
give in order to take possession of his inheritance: "Father Isla also wrote with
a holy purity of intention the most useful satires, which the perversity of the
mob transformed into punishable libels." This is what Valentín Gómez wrote
me seventeen years ago, and this will be the thesis I hope to develop before
you, with one modification. Because it is not necessary, in my judgment, to
appeal ceremoniously to human *perversity* to explain the malice of certain acts;
the *foolishness* of humanity is enough to explain its committing certain actions
that have the appearance and even the responsibility of true crimes.

Coloma wrote about Father Francisco José de Isla for two reasons. First,
Valentín Gómez, the man who in life had defended him and in death
had ceded his academy chair to him, had praised Isla's useful satire,
likening it to *Bagatelles.* For Coloma this was a providential act, and
providence's surrogate Luis Coloma would show his gratitude by talking on Isla. Second, Coloma sees several parallels between Isla and
himself. Isla had his expulsion of 1767 and Coloma his revolution of
1868. Isla was the satirist of the miserable world he lived in, and
Coloma the satirist of "our epoch, pessimistic and misanthropic." Isla's
book was suppressed by the Inquisitors of the Holy Office, and Colo-

ma's criticized by the inquisitors of the unholy office, "the Turkish warship with Christian flag," Restoration Spain. And both were Jesuits who lived part of their lives in exile from Spain. In writing about Francisco José de Isla Coloma was writing about himself, or the Coloma he would like to be.

Chapter Nine
Conclusion

The meaning of Coloma's life may be summed up in two ideas. First, he called himself the "missionary-novelist," a predicant artist who explicitly used his literary talent for spreading the Gospel. This insistent preaching, by constantly revealing the hand of the missionary and isolating many of the readers, had a deleterious effect on his art.[1] Nevertheless, the novelist frequently ignored the missionary, being carried away with his own satire and historical insights, so that no lover of caricature or student of the Restoration can afford to overlook *Bagatelles*. Thus Coloma, the artist in spite of himself, will enjoy some fame within the continuum known as the Spanish novel.

The ultimate significance of his life may be gleaned from a phrase of Ortega y Gasset, who in explaining the modern theme (*El tema de nuestro tiempo*) quotes the words of Christ: "The Sabbath was made for man, man was not made for the Sabbath." Coloma still lived in a rationalist Europe and did not understand this existentialist exegesis. Although he himself did not realize it, he thought that man was made for the Sabbath, to observe all the rules and rituals for a span of years, suffer, die, and then go to heaven. This attitude will account for his stern, Jansenistic morality, and even explain his vision of the missionary-novelist, a figure necessarily lacking vital spontaneity.[2] But humanity and art cannot because they will not be entirely suppressed by the Sabbath and mission. They will always peep out, or burst out, somehow, as Luis Coloma the free man did when he wrote *Bagatelles*.

Appendix One

This appendix contains a letter to Don Luis Alfonso, literary critic of *La Epoca,* that Luis Coloma wrote in answer to criticism of his famous novel *Bagatelles.* The last part of the letter will be clearer if the reader bears in mind that King Alfonso XIII was not quite five years old during the *Bagatelles* controversy of March–April 1891.

My very dear sir,

I have read the two articles you dedicate to me in *La Epoca,* and I find in the second one something I had not found in the first, a blunt and methodical attack, but a loyal attack, that of a gentleman, made face to face and with sword in hand. Therefore, I ought to thank you, and I do thank you; I want to answer you, and I am going to do so, but without attacking you, only defending myself against the extremely grave charges imputed to me, and trying to get across a dangerous reef that you put before me: the necessity of speaking of myself. And I call this reef dangerous, because it is necessary when speaking of oneself to do so well or badly: and the first is always the foolishness of pride, and the second can easily be the silliness of humility.

Lately a flood of letters and newspapers has invaded the solitude I customarily live in because of my ill health, bringing me news of my— why not say it?—unfortunate book, *Bagatelles.* In one of the newspapers, I came across the following observation, which seemed exact to me: "It happens that two people go to a country, they study it, they examine it, they travel all over it in the same manner; and when they go to write about it, instead of being in agreement, from the same data they come to conclusions diametrically opposed. And the truth is that intellects are almost never plain mirrors, but convex or concave, like the ones they exhibit in the stalls of the fairs, and real events take on a certain deformation in the judgment of the reflecting surface. This accounts for the fierce polemics and animated opposition among the. . . , let it be anybody; let us say among the critics who are concerned about *Pequeñeces,* for in my opinion, in many of the mirrors of their respective intellects my book has not reflected the same image it reflected when I created it. Therefore, Mr. Alfonso, may I ask you to please come with me and place yourself as a judge in the same position I was in as author, and we shall see if your intellect, which I recognize as being clear, and your heart, which I am pleased to believe as upright, reflect the same image that my heart and mind conceived when I sketched out the lines of *Pequeñeces*.

A thousand times I have read in books and heard in conversations that Madrid is a mudhole, and I have heard this not from people unfamiliar with society but from the highest part of society itself. But judging from my own experience what I knew about these remarks, which hit the target exactly some times but were temerarious for the most part, and frequently calumnious, I shrugged my shoulders and murmured to myself: this isn't true. Madrid is not a mudhole. . . . There is in the city a mudhole, a small but poisonous leaven that smells rotten . . . that corrupts all of society, imposes its laws and its vices, and makes society appear scandalous to a degree it really isn't. . . . And the awareness of this truth and the knowledge of this injustice made me conceive the plot of *Bagatelles* with the upright, wholesome, and *exclusive* intention of defending society where it deserved to be defended and attacking it for what, in my judgment, is its capital sin and the origin and source of all its deformities: the shameful tolerance of the scandalous, which frees vice of every social sanction that might brand its forehead with a mark of infamy and contain it if not with the fear of God at least with shame and human respect; the shameful tolerance that familiarizes even the most upright consciences with scandal and destroys the powerful barrier of horror and alienation that ought to separate the good man from the scandalous man, and that by making the latter tolerable ends up making him worthy of imitation.

There you have the plan and exclusive goal of *Bagatelles*: to defend the *large majority* against the contagion of the *exiguous number,* and to reproach the former for their lack of foresight and prudence in not fleeing the danger of leprosy. Parallel to these ideas there runs through all the pages of the book another idea that you have understood perfectly; the immense misfortune that the sins of parents bring upon their innocent children, through the terrible and logical connection of natural facts.

According to you, I erred in the procedure I employ for developing my first idea, and lest this be true let us examine it. I gradually followed in the pages of my book the same impressions and effects that happen one after another in the mind of him who observes the world for the first time: there are immediately presented to his sight some outstanding figures, few in number, that grow in his imagination because they appear everywhere on peoples' tongues and in stories, as you nobly and judiciously concede me; then come those other persons who are also in evidence, though upstage somewhat, concealing beneath elegant frivolities or aristocratic haughtiness a simple integrity in many cases, and rather colorless virtue in others. Further upstage, with a deeper look one can see beautiful paradigms, noble characters who are hidden perhaps by the very weight of their good qualities, and these people surprise the observer, who, frightened by what he has already seen, might never have believed them to be so numerous.

Well, this same series of impressions is what I have tried to convey in the pages of *Pequeñeces,* and from the boudoir of the duchess of Bara to the sanctuary of Loyola, the reader has passed through the mud pond I abominate and through the group I sympathize with, until he comes finally to the beautiful figures of the Spanish aristocracy I venerate, as models *not made up by me:* the duchess of Astorga, Genoveva Butrón, the marchioness of Villasis, the marchioness of Sabadell, the marquis of Benhacel, a model of that Alphonsine loyalty which I make fun of according to *those rumors out there,* and the duke of Ordaz, who rejects with noble decorum the pretensions of a nephew who wants to be presented at court. . . .

Have you seen those churches that abound in the little towns of France? The cemetery surrounds them, and in order to arrive at God's sanctuary one must cross the field of the dead; well then, to awaken in the soul of the reader the wholesome impression felt in these churches I took him by the hand in that direction through the pages of *Pequeñeces,* so that he might learn to appreciate all the beauty of what is immortal, contemplating first all the horror of the earthly made dust; all the sweetness of rest, feeling previously all the fatigue of the road; all the tranquillity of virtue operating, without staining itself amongst the whirlpools of vice. . . . That I missed, according to you, the mark and didn't know how to express the complete strength of my idea: well tell me then that the colors of my palette are pale, and the forces of my *well-intentioned wit* lacking, but don't make the mistake of saying that I present only the reverse side of the medal (I believe it may be of Pyramus) and captiously hide the handsome bust standing out on the other side.

And notice that I have said types *not made up by me,* types that I

venerate of the Spanish aristocracy, because this phrase will lead us to
the first of the two serious charges you make in your article: the question of the portraits.

La Epoca itself, in its issue of 23 March, flatly affirms that the
shrewdest observer cannot find in my book one true living portrait,
and so the change produced in public opinion against my novel must
be attributed to the furor with which some people attack my intentions; that is to say, to the rumors and investigations you echo. . . .
And so that's the way things are as a matter of fact: my book appeared
with the sincerest of explanatory footnotes, which I included because
of my knowledge of the terrain; and my book was read, and people
read in it what it said, and they saw in it what should have been seen,
social types and not individual portraits, producing that *general opinion*
so favorable to the distinguished member of the Society of Jesus, which
La Epoca speaks of. . . . But subsequent malice and the crazy Madrid
pruritus of fashioning satires, of giving cruel nicknames, of firing off
bloody ditties, pounced on the book, and, finding the richest of store-
houses in it, notwithstanding my warnings . . . that malice and that
pruritus, together and in common accord, are what have converted the
book—they and not I!—into a pillory which they have tied the victims
to. Notice, if that is not so, how few originals they have found for the
saintly and beautiful figures I present in my book alongside the wicked
figures and caricatures. How few María Villasises they have found by
following the clue of her white hair! How few marquises of Benhacel
they have found, concentrating on his virile countenance; of pure Spanish race and tanned by the sun! . . . And nevertheless these are social
types not individual portraits, just like the others, and in these as in
the others you can also find the feature of white hair, common to thousands of women, or the virile type of the Spanish race, characteristic of
hundreds of men. But this couldn't happen and it hasn't happened,
because malice didn't find any joke in it; folly, always naive and frequently culpable, had nothing to point out and therefore nothing to
believe, to applaud, and to repeat.

What has happened is both foolish and culpable, and your superior
judgment cannot help but recognize that, Mr. Alfonso. Imagine that
I dream up a hunchbacked figure, ugly, repugnant, with a long nose,
and that I baptize him with the name of Peter. Imagine also that a
friend of yours comes to you and says: "And do you think this Peter
fellow is an imaginary figure: Well, you're mistaken: it's John, in the
flesh and blood." "But," you say, "John is graceful and this chap

hunchbacked, he is handsome and the other one ugly, likeable, and the other repugnant, a perfect gentleman and the other a cheating riffraff." "Well, you're mistaken; you're not acquainted with the malicious talent of Father Coloma; this fellow is John, and not Peter." "But how do you know that? What do you base it on?" "Because the flesh and blood John, and Peter as portrayed, both have a long nose: therefore they are one and the same."

Doesn't this strike you as the height of absurdity and ridiculousness, the height of gall and perversity? . . . And don't you think that it is I who have the right to be angry, to protest, to cast away this stupid calumny, which, while converting my book into a pillory with victims lashed to it at the same time stains my priestly condition with the note of libeler?

But my own indignation does not blind me to the point of not understanding that those foolish rumors might have awakened the indignation of others, without any responsibility on my part to be sure; and I want to remedy, *for the sake of charity* what I need not remedy *for the sake of justice.* Therefore, freely and spontaneously, with no pressure whatever from without or within, because this is dictated not by my conscience, which does not oblige me, but by my heart, which will suffer no one to be injured if I can help it—if you know of some respectable person whom that gossip, which you denounce, has offended or bothered, tell me about it in a private letter, and tell me also how, when, where, and in what way the person wants me to satisfy him, because I am prepared to do whatever is necessary to put to rights what I have not offended him with and to defend him against what I have not attacked him with: I shall do anything, from retracting what others have said, in the newspaper of his choice, to ordering the public burning, if that is necessary, of the third printing of *Pequeñeces,* which is being published in all haste at the present time.

But if, as may well be the case, the clamor arises from that mudhole whose existence I denounce and you affirm and even augment; that mudhole where my lash has laid bare positive vices without striking the epidermis of my neighbor—oh!, then, no; then I am not moved to pity, and much less am I intimidated, nor will I retract. Tell them that I stand by everything I have said and that if because of them I wrote *Pequeñeces* with a pen of iron, I am still anxious to write *Monstruosities* with a pen of bronze. . . . And this not for reasons of cruel revenge but for reasons of duty; not out of caprice but conscience; because the novel is my pulpit, and I have the obligation in it of preaching the morality of the gospels, not that of fashionable newspapers; and on the tremendous day when some of the mudhole people will have to gnash their teeth, I don't want it to happen that I will have to gnash mine also, repeating with the temporizing cowardly priest: Woe is me because I spoke not!—*Vae mihi, quia tacui*! . . .

And this, Mr. Alfonso, is the true charity of Jesus Christ, the charity of the prudent man which according to St. Augustine is sweet for some and bitter for others. And know that when you cite in your article the soft words of the Redeemer to the adultress—Nor do I condemn you; go and sin no more—you forgot to emphasize the most important circumstance; that when Jesus Christ pronounced them the sinning woman already had tears in her eyes: and rest assured that if he had seen in her face the angry looks and mocking gestures that you see there and that I descry here in the depths of the mudhole, he would have hurled at her the *Race of vipers*!—which you accuse me of. When the first tear wells up in the eyes of Curra Albornoz, she immediately finds herself in the arms of María Villasis, the strong Christian woman; and in heaven she sees the immense mercy of God which comes forth to meet her with open arms.

This is the terrifying vision I raise before the mudhole I am combatting and the abyss to which the formidable arsenal of *Pequeñeces* pushes all of society, conjuring at the same time exile and dispossession over the head of an innocent child. . . . No, Mr. Alfonso, the point must be very crucial, but it has been overused and has fallen into discredit. The man who has participated in enthusiastic causes of yesteryear does not make fun of them; and you are right to resist believing he does so; nor does the man fire a shot at Alphonsine loyalty who knew how and desired—note this very well—*desired* to trace the figure of the marquis of Benhacel as a living image of the loyalty that shines most, that was sealed with blood on the battlefield. For everyone who has eyes to see, loyalty to King Alfonso is not only respected in all the characters of *Pequeñeces*, even in those who falsify it (as so many did falsify it in those days when I myself was an actor and witness); in the Benhacel family it is, so to speak, *poeticized*.

No, Mr. Alfonso, the exile and dispossession of an innocent boy are not to come from that quarter, and let us hope from no quarter at all. . . . I myself saw him once; his own mother introduced me to him, and when I imagined to myself in his presence the enormous weight that hung over that little head so ignorant still of life, I felt the respectful sadness that the misfortune of an angel would have instilled in me, an angel obliged to descend from heaven in order to take on the most tremendous of human responsibilities. . . . And do you know what happened then? . . . Well, I'm going to tell you, even at the risk of causing laughter. His mother left us alone a long time; an old lady and a young governess were not far removed; and while the child with innocent formality was showing me a doll house, and while he declared with charming self-assurance that the ducks in it were made of brass and weren't real, I, feeling obligated to give that child something of my own, to fortify that august debility with something heavenly, I gave him the only thing I could. On the sly, because it seemed daring to me, I raised my hand above his angelic head, Mr. Alfonso, the sinful hand that was then writing the formidable arsenal of *Pequeñeces*—a puny hand because it belonged to an obscure and until yesterday unknown man, but a great and powerful hand because it has the power of blessing from God himself—and I blessed him.

No, no, Mr. Alfonso, no danger is to come to that innocent child from the formidable arsenal of *Pequeñeces,* nor from the man who wrote it nor from those who, as it has been insidiously suggested, inspired me to write it; for I and I alone am responsible for what I speak and write, and malevolent insinuations with their false accusations cannot succeed in staining the religious order that I love and venerate like a mother. In his happy ignorance that little boy knows nothing of this, but his guardian angel knows it most certainly.

And since I now release my sword never to defend myself again, throw yours aside too, Mr. Alfonso, and give me your hand; for I would consider it an honor to take it. Your most obedient servant in Christ,

Luis Coloma

Appendix Two

The letter in appendix 1 reveals perhaps every side of the author, Luis Coloma, except his love of caricature and satire. One finds an example of his zest for this kind of literature in the following passage, translated from book 2, chapter 2, of *Pequeñeces*. The Diogenes mentioned here is not the Greek philosopher of antiquity, but a cynical, crapulous nobleman whom his contemporaries have nicknamed Diogenes.

Glued, dyed, combed, and glossy by dint of cosmetics, and dancing on the tips of his toes, since his very tight hose allowed him no other mode of walking although it failed to hide two fabled bunions, Uncle Frasquito hastily went out on the terrace, he the universal uncle of the grandees of Spain, and of those their adjutants the nobles of second rank, of the vulgar rich of every cast, of political and literary notabilities, of official loafers, of daring adventurers and anonymous personages who form the *all Madrid* of the court, the ill-matched *dessus du panier*[1] of the great Madrilenian world.

This entire world called him Uncle Frasquito because good style had decreed it so, and he was pleased to accept the kinship of all those whose blue blood was really united, a century sooner or a century later, with his most illustrious own; as for the others, without rejecting the apocryphal nature of their kinship, he placed them with a certain protective condescension in the category of *spurious nephews*.

Uncle Frasquito had stood out in this universal family for half a century, seeing generations and generations of nieces and nephews, legitimate or spurious, parade by; and these were born and grew up, married and multiplied, died and putrefied, but he, shielded behind the tightest of corsets subjecting the insolent rebellion of his abdomen, had never gotten past his thirty-third year; his years, like the weeks of Daniel, were years of years, although, more accommodating than the weeks, they expanded or contracted as the circumstances saw fit. He counted thirty-three when in the year forty he attended the wedding of the queen of England, accompanying the extraordinary envoy of the court of Spain, and he counted the very same when in 1853 he saw the wedding of his *niece* Eugenia de Guzmán to the emperor Napoleon III;

an unequal marriage, a humiliating *messa allianza* that Uncle Frasquito absolutely disapproved, for he wasn't entirely satisfied with Bonaparte's lineage, and although he never came to relegate his new nephew to the category of the spurious ones, neither would he designate him by any other name than "my nephew the Count Consort of Teba."[2]

Legend whispered the Uncle Frasquito carried on his body thirty-two prosthetic parts, among which was numbered a cork buttocks. It is certain, as we introduce him to our readers, that as he was returning from the Jouffroy trip where he was verifying the duke of Aosta's[3] abdication for his compatriots, obesity had changed his palm tree waist into a cooking pot from Alcorcón, and that art, industry, and even mechanics were working jointly in the daily restoration of that stale old Narcissus, who always ran the risk of becoming a Swiss chard, just as the ancient Narcissus of Greek mythology became a flower.

Uncle Frasquito was a bachelor, a rich man; he lived in orderly fashion, he had no known vices, nor debts either; he was affable, courteous, helpful, obliging; he had the manners of a bashful maiden and the cadences in his voice of a presumptuous debutante. He collected diplomatic seals, he embroidered tapestries, he played the flute disastrously, and he pronounced his *r*'s in that guttural and drawn-out style peculiar to Parisians, whom some elegant Frenchified Spaniards imitate; and this is a natural defect in many others, for whom they have invented the saying: "El perro de San Roque no tiene rabo, porque Ramón Ramírez se lo ha robado."[4]

Diogenes usually called him Francesca di Rimini, and at times *señá* Frasquita, and he was wont to pursue him and harass him with untimely embraces through drawing rooms and living rooms, and even among the ladies' skirts, where the effeminate nobleman liked to take refuge; with embraces that wrinkled and soiled his immaculate shirtfront; with extemporaneous kisses that obliged the neat victim to wash himself and rub himself with cold cream; with furtive foot thrusts that dirtied his stockings and made his bunions explode, or with bestial handshakes that disjointed his fingers, putting him in danger of spreading about on all sides the thirty-two components legend assigned to his body.

Those two old men, of such diverse character and customs, were straggling types of the same society, two exemplary fossils of those noblemen of the last century, vicious and cynical sassy boys some of them, effeminate dandies the others, both of whom paved the way for the ruin and discredit of the Spanish grandees.

Well then, Uncle Frasquito came into the terrace with the air of a maiden in distress, and everybody crowded around him, assailing him with questions. . . . Everything, but everything was confirmed by other sources, and in Madrid it was a general case of *sauve qui peut* . . . ! !⁵

The news was corroborated that King Amadeo had fled to Lisbon with his family, and the telegraph was wiring the names of those individuals who were to form the first ministry of the newly born republic.

"Of the Spanish Rrrepublic!," exclaimed Uncle Frasquito, removing his hat with burlesque solemnity.

And among the scornful laughs and ironical observations, he began to read from his elegant little notebook, where he had written down the names of the new ministers. . . . But what names, Most Holy Virgin! If it wasn't enough to make you die of laughter! . . . Figueras, Castelar, Pi y Margall, the two Salmerón brothers, Nicolás and Paquito. . . . Córdoba.

"Córrrrdoba, ladies and gentlemen, Córrrdoba! . . . Ferrrnandito Córrrdoba, rrrepublicano! . . . Who would believe it, when we went together to the Benavente palace when Fernando VII sent him to Portugal with his brother Luis, after the prince Don Carlos and the Princess of Beyrra! . . . Of courrrse, I was then only a child, a trrrue creaturrre. . . ."

Uncle Frasquito did not realize that according to this data he must have attended the soirées of the duchess of Benavente six years before he was born. . . .

Notes and References

Preface

1. *Pequeñeces,* ed. Rubén Benítez (Madrid: Ediciones Cátedra, 1975). The forty-page introduction by Benítez is one of the most discerning criticisms I have seen, and his footnotes throw light on many passages.
2. *Obras completas,* 4th ed. (Madrid: Razón y Fe, 1960).
3. *Boy* (Mexico City: Ed. Porrúa, 1966).

Chapter One

1. According to Emilia Pardo Bazán, one Jesuit was severely censured for preaching a message similar to Coloma's; see her *El P. Luis Coloma* (Madrid: Sáenz de Jubera, 1891). 19–20.
2. Pardo Bazán thought Coloma the novelist best equipped to write about high society "from within." See ibid., 24–25, 56. See also the Marqués de Figueroa, "La novela aristocrática," *La España Moderna* 3 (1891):53–65. Coloma's *Bagatelles* was preferred, for example, to José María de Pereda's *La Montálvez* (1888), Armando Palacio Valdés's *La espuma* (1891), and the Marqués de Figueroa's *La vizcondesa de armas* (1887). For the dedication to the duke of Luna, see *OC,* 668.
3. Coloma borrowed this expression from the French traditionalist, Louis Veuillot, whom he mentions several times in his works. One critic, Emilio Bobadilla, accused Coloma of an uncommon use of Gallicisms, for example, the use of *avalancha* instead of *alud* for *avalanche*; the use of *sufrir* instead of *padecer* in a sentence like "Castropardo sufrió otro acceso de hilaridad" and the use of *revancha* for *revenge.* See Emilio Bobadilla ("Fray Candil"), *El P. Coloma y la aristocracia* (Madrid, 1891), 57–80.
4. Since the revolutionary junta at Jerez included the mercurial Andalusian republican, José Paúl y Angulo, who was later accused of assassinating General Prim, the events in Jerez may have been exceptionally bitter for a traditionalist like Coloma.
5. For some references to Pellico, see *OC,* 432, 884, 1361. On *OC,* 401, he remembers a minute detail from *My Years In Prison.* On *OC,* 1361, the names of Thomas à Kempis, Fernán Caballero, and Silvio Pellico form a kind of trinity.
6. See Silvio Pellico, *Mis prisiones* (Buenos Aires: Espasa-Calpe, 1945), 187.
7. Apparently the reception in Italy of *My Years In Prison* was similar

to that of *Bagatelles* in Spain. See Pellico, *Mis prisiones*, 187, where he mentions the fanatics of two opposing factions.

8. See Rafael Hornedo's prologue to Coloma's *Obras completas*, xxiv. Following Hornedo's lead, Joaquín Antonio Peñalosa has also called it "the mysterious event": see the prologue to *Boy*, xi.

9. See Genaro Cavestany, *Memorias de un sesentón sevillano* (Sevilla: F. Díaz, 1918), 1:113–22.

10. Writing in 1891, Pardo Bazán says: "Some people attributed the event to mysterious causes; but the best-informed persons assure that Coloma wounded himself involuntarily, while cleaning a firearm in his room. Be that as it may . . ." (*El P. Luis Coloma*, 15).

11. Benito Pérez Galdós devoted his sixth series of *National Episodes* to this period of Spanish history. One of these novels is called *Spain Without a King*.

12. See the prologue to *OC*, xxxiii.

13. In a duel Alarcón's opponent fired his pistol into the air, Alarcón was so impressed that he experienced a religious conversion.

14. See Avery Dulles, *Testimony to Grace* (New York: Sheed Ward, 1946), in which the author describes his conversion.

15. C. W. Lewis tells of his conversion in *Surprised By Joy* (London: G. Bles, 1955).

16. See *Epistolario del P. Luis Coloma* (Santander: Imprenta Provincial, 1947), 93, 123, 138.

17. Coloma never explicitly mentions Renan, the French clergyman who denied Christ's miracles and divinity in the *Life of Jesus* (1863), but in a story about miracles, *Un milagro*, he speaks of "a certain foreign academician" and "his profound Orientalist studies," and he uses French words in scorning the doctrines of this academician (*risée publique, enfant terrible*); moreover, he admires the French Catholic, Louis Veuillot, who answered Renan with another *Life of Jesus* (1864). Nor does he mention Draper, whose *History of the Conflict Between Religion and Science* appeared in 1875, or his own colleague Father Miguel Mir, S. J., who before he left the Jesuits answered Draper with his book-length essay, *The Harmony Between Science and Faith*. Coloma does not mention these influential authors by name, but the reader can detect their presence in his repeated defense of his religion and the Jesuit order.

18. Rubén Benítez, quoting Brian Dendle, makes an interesting observation: "There is, however, a clear relation between Coloma and the previous novel, but specifically that novel coming from popular literature, the social serial novels. Dendle observes that behind all the religious literature of that period there is to be found, either by acceptance or by rejection, *The Wandering Jew* of Eugène Sue" (see Benítez's introduction to *Pequeñeces*, 33). Pardo Bazán, in *El P. Luis Coloma*, says that Christian literature should not be concerned

only "with the eternal refutation of Draper and the case against liberalism" (101).

19. *Bagatelles* constituted *toutes proportions gardées* a sort of Dreyfuss affair in Spanish letters. The literary public was split not by the fate of an innocent man opposite French traditionalism but by the fate of Spanish traditionalism and liberalism opposite each other.

20. Pedro Antonio de Alarcón's novel *Scandal* (1875) and Benito Pérez Galdós's play *Electra* (1901) had a reception similar to that of *Bagatelles* (1891). The reader interested in the *Bagatelles* affair should consult the following authors in the bibliography: Federico Balart, Arvède Barine, Emilio Bobadilla, Rafael Hornedo, M. Martínez Barrionuevo, Emilia Pardo Bazán, and Juan Valera.

21. The former Jesuit, Miguel Mir, voted for him, the dissenting ballot belonging probably to Octavio Picón. See Rafael Hornedo's prologue, in the *OC*, lxxxvi.

22. I have translated Coloma's Academy speech on Father Isla and deposited two manuscript copies with the librarian at the University of Wisconsin–Milwaukee. This translation has not been published.

23. See *OC*, lxxxvi.

24. See *Pequeñeces; Jeromín* (Mexico City: Ed. Porrúa, 1972); this is the second edition of the Porrúa *Pequeñeces*, the first edition having appeared in 1968. See also Benítez' edition of *Pequeñeces*.

Chapter Two

1. The sacred vessels of *Half John and John and a Half* bring to mind Gustavo Adolfo Bécquer's *La ajorca de oro* (The golden bracelet), where the young lover loses his mind after stealing jewels in church from the Virgin. A masterful teller of tales, Bécquer adds no commentary of any kind, let alone an explanation, for none is needed.

2. This "certain foreign academician" can only be Ernest Renan, the French ex-clergyman whose *Life of Jesus* scandalized Europe in 1863. Renan argued that Jesus was not God and that he did not perform miracles.

3. This I should say is the main difficulty with all of Coloma's stories: they are overly didactic, they lack nuance, and the narrator tends to isolate the good reader from other, presumably perverse, readers.

4. Coloma's stories "What Could It Be?" and "The Blue Salon" most resemble the *Contes Cruels* of Villiers de L'Isle-Adam. The Frenchman also uses letters with asterisks for persons and places (D***), and the preternatural atmosphere he creates seems to be a model for Coloma. In any case, the latter employs French expressions constantly and German words very rarely.

5. The only other evidence of such a style is in the story "¡¡Chist!!"

(*OC,* 278) and the *Memories of Fernán Caballero* (*OC,* 1360). In another story, *First Letters: Two Johns,* he refers to the Scholastics (*OC,* 412).
    6. My colleague, Pierre Ullman, suggests the following translation:

> St. Louis, of France the king,
> was to God so wont to cling
> that, to make of him a saint,
> God forgave his Frenchman's taint.

    7. Concerning "the problem of the book and of its influence on life," see Leo Spitzer, "On the Significance of *Don Quijote,*" *Modern Language Notes* 77 (1962):113–29. See also Miguel de Cervantes, *Don Quixote,* ed. Martín de Riquer (Barcelona: Ed. Juventud, 1958), and Mariano José de Larra, "Casarse pronto y mal," in *Artículos de costumbres* (Madrid: Espasa-Calpe, 1952), 1:60–73.
    8. Coloma advocates what Etienne Gilson has called "the primacy of faith." Gilson writes a paragraph that seems singularly appropriate for judging Coloma's didactic stories and their allegedly historical demonstrations: "If it is of the essence of an article of faith to rest upon divine authority alone, its would-be demonstrations cannot be necessary demonstrations. Now our faith in Revelation should not be a merely natural assent to some rational probability. When something is rationally probable, its contrary also is rationally probable. It is but an opinion. Religious faith is not an opinion. It is the unshakable certitude that God has spoken, and that what God has said is true, even though we do not understand it. Hence Thomas Aquinas' repeated warnings not to overrate the value of such probabilities, lest, as he himself says, 'the Catholic faith seem to be founded on empty reasonings, and not, as it is, on the most solid teaching of God.' And again: 'it is useful to consider this, lest anyone, presuming to demonstrate what is of faith, should bring forth reasons that are not cogent, so as to give occasion to unbelievers to laugh, and to think that such are the grounds on which we believe things that are of faith' (*Reason and Revelation in the Middle Ages* [New York: Scribner's 1966], 77).

Chapter Three

    1. I am using Benítez's edition of *Pequeñeces.*
    2. This statement will show the spirit of Coloma's *Portraits of Yore* and the *Marquis de Mora,* which study the fops and cynics of the eighteenth century. *Portraits of Yore* supposedly tells the story of a saintly woman, but Coloma devotes much of the book to her vicious relatives.
    3. The art of the *esperpento,* which one might call scarecrow art in English, has been likened to a distorting mirror outside a jewelry store in Madrid where the passerby sees himself now excessively tall and thin, now short and fat, with misshapen head, hands, and feet, much like the mirrors everyone

has seen at a circus. The chief practitioner of this art was Ramón del Valle-Inclán (1866–1936), whose gnostic satirical *esperpentos* stand in the first rank of modern Spanish literature. It may seem odd to call Coloma, the Jesuit priest, a modest precursor of Valle-Inclán, the sacrilegious anti-Jesuit, but such is the case. Coloma the missionary Christian had as little in common with Valle, the missionary anti-Christian, as one can possibly have, but in their fondness for the grotesque they share a common sympathy. Valle attributes his joy in the grotesque to the gnosticism he professes in his aesthetic grammar, *La lámpara maravillosa* (The Wonderful Lamp) whereas for Coloma gnosticism is a repugnant system, especially when it leads to sacrilege. Nevertheless, both men take delight in deforming a character and leaving him in a ridiculous state, like a naked skull or winter melon. Luis Coloma's declamatory prose has not received the acclamation of Valle's musical prose in the latter's *sonata-esperpento, Tirano Banderas,* but he perceived something in the air that Valle did also, a deformation of the human spirit, which he captured in certain pages of *Bagatelles.*

4. The syntax of the first sentence of book 2, chapter 7 of *Bagatelles* is complicated, and in my English translation I have omitted a clause and a series of possessive pronouns of doubtful antecedents. Coloma's critics often accused him of a careless style, although one of them saw a natural charm in it. In the bibliography see the studies of Emilio Bobadilla and Federico Balart.

5. Coloma's Father Cifuentes brings to mind Pedro Antonio de Alarcón's Father Manrique, in his thesis novel *Scandal.* Both *Bagatelles* (1891) and *Scandal* (1875) caused a furor in Spain.

6. A translation of Dante's verses: "No greater sorrow / than remembering happy times/ in the midst of misery"; of Santillana's verses: "The greatest sorrow / that any lover can have / is to remember joy / in the time of sorrow."

7. "The customs . . . were probably not admirable ": The following quotation, from Jacinto Benavente's memoirs, concerns the years 1866 to 1886: "The *entretenidas* [entertaining women] that's what they called them then, were an ornament of the stroll and of Madrilenian life. Almost all of them were known not by their names, which never were their real names, but by the title of the house of whose ostentation and wealth they were a part. Public morality was not alarmed the least bit by these exhibitions. Jesuitism did not rule yet: *that one should not see the smoke even though the house is burning;* then the smoke was of such an attractive appearance, that it was not possible to hide where the house was burning. On the promenades, in the theaters, at the bull fights, at the races, at every kind of public entertainment, the *entretenidas* came across and rubbed elbows with the wives of their *entretenidos* (entertainers), who, far from looking at them with hatred or scorn, took pride in seeing them so well displayed" (*Recuerdos y olvidos* [Madrid: Aguilar, 1962], 255). *Entretenidos* may also be translated as "the men entertained." Perhaps it is best to translate *entretenidas* as "kept women" and *entretenidos* as "keepers."

8. Bobadilla, *El P. Coloma y la aristocracia,* 12.

9. There is some biffy humor in Coloma's Cinderella story, "¡Ajajú!," in which the doll Rafaela gives money to Mariquita and *caca* (excrement) to her stepsisters. The king later has the doll glued permanently to his buttocks. (See *OC,* 469.)

10. See Vincente de la Fuente, *Historia de las sociedades secretas y especialmente de la francmasonería,* 2 vol. (Lugo: Imprenta de Soto Freire, 1881), 2:316.

11. There is a copy of *La araña negra* at UCLA and possibly elsewhere. The novel was originally published as two volumes, but in the edition at UCLA it appears as ten books in three volumes.

12. Coloma's *Bagatelles* resembled Alarcón's thesis novel, *Scandal,* and Blasco Ibàñez's *The Black Spider* resembled Eugène Sue's *The Wandering Jew,* in which the Jesuits appear as villains. Thus the two novels belong to two traditions in nineteenth-century literature, both of them aware of the other. For example, Coloma brings up *The Wandering Jew* in book 4, chapter 1 of *Bagatelles.*

13. See Pardo Bazán, *El P. Luis Coloma,* 116–118.

14. See P. Francisco Blanco García, *La literatura española en el siglo XIX,* 2d pt., 3d ed. (Madrid: Sáenz de Jubera, 1910), 472.

15. This statement and the one alluded to in note 19 are to be found in Francisco Blanco García and in the article on Coloma in the *Enciclopedia Ilustrada.*

16. See Bobadilla, *El P. Coloma y la aristocracia,* 57–79, for a list of scores of examples of assonances and consonances found in Coloma's prose.

17. The reader should consult Ceferino Suárez Bravo, *España demagógica* (Madrid: Imprenta de Antonio Pérez Dubrull, 1873), where he will see the same *fango* style as in Coloma; Suárez Bravo writes: "There is nothing that seduces the common people like novelty. Therefore, the stirrers of social mud (*fango*) take so much care in making people believe that all modern revolutions come pregnant with some new thing" (9). Suárez Bravo goes on to speak of "los fondos cenagosos de la sociedad española," "lodo," and the Masons. Thus Coloma's use of *fango, cenagal, asqueroso,* and so forth comes from the standard antirevolutionary rhetoric of his day.

18. Bobadilla, *El P. Coloma y la aristocracia,* 79.

19. Federico Balart, *Impresiones* (Madrid: Librería de Fernando Fe, 1894), 248. See also Pardo Bazán, *El P. Luis Coloma,* 116–18.

20. The history behind the creation of *Bagatelles* is this: In the late 1870s and 1880s Coloma felt himself being drawn more and more to the novel, and specifically, to the thesis novel. His deceased friend Fernán Caballero had set him an example, which he strove to imitate with his inchoate pastiche *Juan Miseria* (John Poverty, 1873); he revised this book and published it in the October 1888 issue of the *Sacred Heart Messenger.* In the meantime, Pedro Antonio de Alarcón published *El escándalo,* (Scandal 1875), a novel

concerning a Jesuit confessor and the redemption of a wayward aristocrat. This volume was a "bookstore success," or best-seller, as we call it today, one of the greatest in Spanish literature. And the dean of Spanish novelists, Benito Pérez Galdós, was publishing two or more novels every year, among them the novels of religious thesis, *Doña Perfecta* (1876) and *Gloria* (1876–77). Galdós's own friend José María Pereda attempted to refute the thesis of these books, which criticized the church, with a novel criticizing agnosticism, *De tal palo tal astilla* (A chip off the old block, 1880). Coloma was also attracted to the French novelists of the day, especially Emile Zola and Alphonse Daudet, whose thesis novel *The Nabob* has been compared to his own *Bagatelles.*

If Coloma were to write a thesis novel (Spanish: *novela de tesis*; French: *roman à thèse*) it would concern that part of church moral doctrine he felt most strongly about, scandal, "the reprehensible word or deed leading to the spiritual ruin of one's neighbor." And in such a novel the scandalous conduct would occur within the society he knew best both before and after his entrance into the Society of Jesus, namely, the aristocracy. Efforts were being made at the time to write the so-called "aristocratic novel"; by the marquis of Figueroa with *La vizcondesa de Armas,* Pereda with *La Montálvez* (1888), and Armando Palacio Valdés with *La espuma* (Foam, 1891); but these books were not favorably received by contemporary critics. Pardo Bazán declared that *La Montálvez* (The Montalvez Woman) errs in its trajectory and hits "as the saying goes, one on the nail and a hundred on the horseshoe." And the marquis of Figueroa, who wrote an article in 1891 called "The Aristocratic Novel," stated in *La España Moderna* 2 (1891):58:

Thus Pereda in *The Montálvez Woman,* showing another charming display of his talents, produced another overdressed picture that might be exact in its details but is not so in its entirety. He accumulated in one lone figure errors, aberrations, and irregularities that could be true in isolation; but joined together they border on the implausible, and above all they depart from the truth itself.

Mr. Palacio Valdés was mistaken to write an aristocratic novel. Mrs. Pardo Bazán herself, as a novelist, hesitates to enter that world and has only made some very light attempts; the illustrious Galdós also only treated it incidentally and as it were from the side. The renowned don Juan Valera is very well acquainted with the *grand monde* and frequently deals with it, but this literary dilettante, this outstanding writer, who is so much in vogue, has stopped writing novels. Those that he has written already belong to another age; this is not then the place to judge them.

Of all our aristocratic novels, *Bagatelles* is the most exact and faithful in its portrayal of persons and things, the most distinguished and typical in its tone and general character, which fits in marvelously with the aristocratic class.

The thesis novel and the "aristocratic novel" were in the air and Coloma was destined to bring them together. Some of his contemporaries sensed this, for they were encouraging him to write *la novela grande*, the full-length novel, several years before the appearance of *Bagatelles*, but no one had the slightest notion of what such a novel might do. No one foresaw the tumult (*algarada*).
21. See Pardo Bazán, *El P. Luis Coloma*, 54.
22. Bobadilla, *El P. Coloma, la aristocracia*, 5–6. More than 50,000 copies of *Bagatelles* were sold in 1891, a record for that era.

Chapter Four

1. The reader of English literature will find some similarities between *Boy* and Evelyn Waugh's *Brideshead Revisited*: an older man recalls his youth, his beautiful young friends, and their Arcadian days together, and then there is death. Boy's "Atame, señor, y ten piedad de mí" (Bind me, Oh Lord, and have mercy on me) is similar to the narrator's study of divine grace in *Brideshead*, where the errant Lord Marchmain and his family are all brought back by adversity to religious truth; moreover, Coloma's social and political preferences, and his satirical vein, are like Waugh's.
2. The Spanish novelist, Antonio de Hoyos y Vinent, has said that when he was a young man Coloma asked him to finish *Boy*. See Hoyos y Vinent, *El primer estado* (Madrid: Renacimiento, 1931), 151–58.
3. See Carlton Joseph Huntley Hayes, *A Generation of Materialism, 1871–1900* (New York: Harper & Brothers, 1941).

Chapter Five

1. The saintly María Pignatelli bears a strong resemblance to the Marchioness María Villasis of *Bagatelles*, the great lady whose dominating presence sets an example for others to follow.
2. In the novel *Boy*, Xavier de Baza (Boy) was lustful; and in *Bagatelles* Currita Albornoz was lustful in the extreme; but both they and Villahermosa were saved through the action of divine grace, which they could accept because they had faith.
3. These words of Benavente throw a great deal of light on modern Spain. The critics have generally pointed to writers like Pío Baroja, Miguel de Unamuno, and Ramón del Valle-Inclán as the revealers of falseness and hypocrisy in their country; Baroja in *The Tree of Knowledge* and Valle in works such as *The Court of Miracles* and *A Trick in Swords* (or *Spades, Baza de espadas*) are especially devastating when it comes to *señoritos achulados*. But this accomplishment of the Generation of 1898 should not lead to a misunderstanding of the conservative opposition, which was also concerned about the Spanish character. A man like Coloma, who represented for the ninety-eighters all that was undesirable in the old Spanish *casticismo* (essence), was also concerned about what was happening to Spain. The Generation of 1898 criticized reli-

gious values they considered to be outworn, values that Coloma staunchly defended, but he no less than they was concerned about dandies, *chulos* and *majos*. Benavente's words are particularly disconcerting: the king of Spain was a caricature, a Teddy Boy!

4. There is some mystery concerning the two little hearts. In a letter to the duchess of Villahermosa, dated 21 June, 1892, Coloma writes: "I would like you, if you remember to do so and it's not too much trouble, to bring to Juin so that I might see them, those little things that you told me you had found of your great-grandmother, and above all, those two little hearts joined by a chain. Lately I have read the will of Mlle. de Lespinasse very slowly, and I believe that the aforesaid little hearts are the same ones that she describes there and left to the duchess of Villahermosa." Coloma is faithful to detail. See *Epistolario del P. Luis Coloma,* 83.

Chapter Six

1. See *Obras completas,* 19 vols. (Madrid: Razón y Fe, 1940–42), 19:94.
2. See Alberto y Arturo García Carraffa, *El Padre Coloma* (Madrid: Imprenta de Juan Pueyo, 1918), 132–33.
3. These are the words of the historian, Van der Hammen, whom Coloma frequently follows. I have taken them from the article on Don John of Austria in *Diccionario de Historia de España* (Madrid: Revista de Occidente, 1952), 2:123.

Chapter Seven

1. Professor Javier Herrero questions the veracity of this episode in "El testimonio del Padre Coloma sobre Fernán Caballero," *Bulletin of Hispanic Studies* 41 (1964):40–50.
2. In chapter 34 (*OC,* 1462) Coloma puns with the surname Montpensier: "Y vea usted lo que son las cosas. . . . Mi padre nunca me decía: '*Ah Montpensier,*' sino '*Mondépensier.*' "
3. See Javier Herrero "El Testimonio," 40–41.
4. Ibid., 46–47. See also the studies of Theodor Heinermann, whom Herrero quotes.

Chapter Eight

1. John Bull: in Spanish, Pero Grullo, A *perogrullada* is a truism.
2. There is a Spanish paperback translation of Louis XIV, the *Memorias sobre el arte de gobernar* (Buenos Aires: Espasa-Calpe, Austral, 1947). José Martínez Ruiz's (Azorín) tract *El político* (The politician), 3d ed. (Madrid: Espasa-Calpe, 1968) resembles Coloma's *Spiritual Exercises for the King Don Alfonso XIII.*

3. I wrote these lines before reading the following passage in P. Hornedo's biography of Coloma: "To this historical work one would have to add today the last and most lamentable chapter, which would have this title: 'On how these relics perished on 11 May 1931, in the burning by the mobs of the church on Flor Street' " (*OC*, lxxxii). In my own text I have left my original statement about *whenever*, because that is the impression the inscription makes on the reader.

Chapter Nine

1. One cannot help but think of Coloma's contemporary, Mark Twain (1835–1910), who wrote this notice at the head of *Huckleberry Finn*: "Persons attempting to find a motive in this narrative will be prosecuted; persons attempting to find a moral in it will be banished; persons attempting to find a plot in it will be shot. . . . By Order of the Author." Coloma the missionary is the opposite of Twain.

2. To paraphrase the Bible: Coloma was saying in effect that "Art was made for the mission." When he follows this dictum his allegedly inspirational works are uninspiring; when he ignores it, they animate the reader.

Appendix Two

1. *Dessus du panier*: the refuse. I have preserved Coloma's French here, since his characters frequently drop French phrases.

2. The Spanish lady Eugenia de Guzmán, wife of Napoleon III, was the countess of Teba.

3. King Amadeo, the Italian who attempted to found a dynasty in Spain, was in Italy the duke of Aosta. The supporters of Alfonso, refusing to recognize his reign, would naturally refer to him as a duke.

4. This is rather like "Peter Piper picked a peck of pickled peppers," emphasizing the *r* rather than the *p*.

5. *Sauve qui peut*: every man for himself. There were rumors of a bloodbath in Madrid, which of course did not take place. By overdramatizing the events in Spain, Tío Frasquito and others make themselves look even more ridiculous.

Selected Bibliography

PRIMARY SOURCES

1. Collected Editions

Obras completas. 19 vols. Madrid: Razón y Fe, 1940–42. The contents of volume 19 do not appear in the other editions of the complete works. This volume, titled *Relieves y crítica,* contains nine letters Coloma wrote to José Pereda, Doña Emilia Pardo Bazán, and others, and forty letters sent him by Fernán Caballero, Gertrudis de Avellaneda, Pereda, Pardo Bazán, and Conrado Muiños Sáenz. It also contains Emilia Pardo Bazán's *Padre Luis Coloma,* Juan Valera's fictitious letter, "Currita Albornoz al Padre Luis Coloma," and Constancio Eguía Ruiz's *El Padre Luis Coloma: Su vocación literaria.*

Obras completas. 2d ed. Madrid: Razón y Fe, 1947. The long prologue by Constancio Eguía Ruiz also appears in Eguía Ruiz's *Literatura y literatos.*

Obras completas. 3d ed. Madrid: Razón y Fe, 1952. The editor is again Constancio Eguía Ruiz.

Obras completas. 4th ed. Madrid: Razón y Fe, 1960. The prologue is a book-length biography by Rafael María de Hornedo.

Pequeñeces; Jeromín. Mexico City: Editorial Porrúa, 1972. Contains instructive prologue and bibliography.

2. Novels and Other Writings

Boy. Mexico City: Editorial Porrúa, 1966. Contains an instructive prologue and bibliography.

Boy. Edited by Myron B. Deily. New York: Bruce Publishing Co., 1934. A students' edition containing many end notes and a Spanish-English vocabulary. Some passages of *Boy* have been omitted.

Epistolario. Edited by Luis Fernández. Santander: Imprenta Provincial, 1947. Contains Coloma's letters to the duchess of Villahermosa and her family, from 1890 to 1914. The letters to the duchess mainly concern Coloma's *El marqués de Mora,* a biography of her great-grandfather. The letters to her husband, the duke, concern the *Pequeñeces* affair.

Pequeñeces. Buenos Aires: Editorial Sopena, 1946. 2d ed., 1950.

Pequeñeces. Edited by Rubén Benítez. Madrid: Ediciones Cátedra, 1975. The forty-page introduction by Benítez is one of the most discerning criticisms I have seen, and his footnotes throw light on many passages. Good bibliography.

3. English Translations

Currita, Countess of Albornoz: A Novel of Madrid Society. Translated by Estelle
Huyck Attwell. Boston: Little Brown, 1900. Translation of *Pequeñeces.*
The First Mass and Other Stories. Translated by E. M. Brookes. Philadelphia:
H. L. Kilner & Co., 1892. Contains eight of Coloma's stories.
John Poverty. Translated by E. M. Brookes. Philadelphia: H. L. Kilner & Co.,
1911. Translation of *Juan Miseria.*
Pérez the Mouse. Adapted from the Spanish by Lady Moreton. New York: John
Lane, 1915. 2d ed. New York: Dodd, Mead, 1950. Translation of *Ratón
Pérez.*
The Story of Don John of Austria. Translated by Lady Moreton. New York: John
Lane, 1912. Translation of *Jeromín.*
A True Hidalgo. Translated by Harold Binns. St. Louis: Herder, n.d. Trans-
lation of *Boy.*

4. French Translations

Bagatelles. Translated by Camilla Vergniol; preface by Marcel Prevost. Paris:
A. Lemerre, 1893. Prevost argues that although Coloma was disen-
chanted with the Restoration, which did not reestablish the church in
Spain, this political question was not his principal concern. He says that
all of the former students of the company will recognize Father Coloma's
doctrine in the Jesuit teaching: "Do not compromise with the world; it
is necessary to live in it with a different rule, one that is also as strict and
binding as that of a religious in his cloister." This will account for the
stern conduct of the marchioness of Villasis, Coloma's spokesman, in
Bagatelles.

Notes: (1) The bibliography of Antonio Palau y Dulcet, *Manual del librero
hispanoamericano* (Madrid: Antonio Palau, 1950), vol. 3, lists the following entry for Luis Coloma: *Vida de San Fernando* (Madrid: Editorial Vol-
untad, 1928). This book, however, was the work of another author, Jesús
Rubio Coloma. (2) Luis Coloma did not live to finish *Fray Francisco,* his
biography of Cardinal Cisneros; it was finished by another Jesuit, Alberto
Risco, after Coloma's death. Although this second part is included in
volume 18 of Coloma's *Obras completas* of 1940–42, it is not to be found
in subsequent editions. Alberto Risco's book is listed in the secondary
sources.

SECONDARY SOURCES

Alas, Leopoldo (Clarín). *Ensayos y revistas, 1888–1892.* Madrid: Manuel Fernández y Lasanta, 1892, 325–29. Says chapter 2 of *Pequeñeces* is worthy

of a master; the rest is poor. Professes warm feelings for Coloma as a person.

Alcalá-Galiano, Alvaro. *Figuras excepcionales.* Madrid: Renancimiènto, 1930, 145–53. As a young student the author became friendly with an older Father Coloma. He learned that *Boy* was censored and "mutilated." This was a source of great sorrow to Coloma, who would change the subject whenever *Boy* was brought up.

Balart, Federico. *Impresiones.* Madrid: Librería de Fernando Fe, 1894, 239–62. Argues that Coloma must be judged separately as a novelist and as a moralist. His moral posture, isolation ("the Marquesa de Villasis will be at home for honorable women and decent gentlemen"), is a social impossibility. Argues that Coloma is adept at narrating action but poor at creating characters.

Balseiro, José A. *Novelistas españoles modernos.* New York: Macmillan Co., 1933, 328–47. Concentrates on *Pequeñeces,* the condemnatory language of which "is not only anti-Christian for its cruelty; its barracks' rudeness also conflicts with the sweetness of the Shepherd." From the literary viewpoint, "the first thing that disgusts us in *Pequeñeces* is its *redaction,* for we will not call the often incorrect, imprecise prose a style."

Barine, Arvède. "Un Jesuite Romancier, Le Père Luis Coloma." *Revue Bleue* 49 (1892):801–6. A study of *Pequeñeces,* written after the news of its sensational success reached France. Calls Coloma the fin de siècle missionary.

Barja, Cesar. *Libros y autores modernos: Siglos XVIII y XIX.* Los Angeles: Campbell's Book Store, 1933. Brief discussion of Coloma. Concludes that *Pequeñeces* is subordinated to a religious and moral rather than an artistic end.

Benalúa, Conde de. *Memorias.* Madrid: Editorial Pueyo, 1924. Throws light on the historical background of the Restoration.

Blanco García, P. Francisco. *La literatura española en el siglo XIX.* Pt. 2. 2d ed. Madrid: Sáenz de Jubera, 1910. Chapter 4 shows the traditionalists' attitude toward Spain and the Restoration; chapter 25 contains many bibliographical references and a favorable review of *Pequeñeces.*

Bobadilla, Emilio ("Fray Candil"). *El P. Coloma y la aristocracia.* Madrid: Sucesores de Rivadeneyra, 1891. An eighty-page criticism for the *Pequeñeces* polemic of 1891. Pages 1–45 and 57–80 are a fine study of the characters, action, dialogue, and style of Coloma's novel; for example, they examine gallicisms, assonant rhyme, *ripios* (padding), and cacophony. Pages 46–56 are an attack on the Jesuits, "most immoral and hypocritical people" who commit *loyoladas.* Thus Bobadilla's study typifies the entire *Pequeñeces* affair: able reasoning coupled with passionate broadsides.

Cavestany, Genaro. *Memorias de un sesentón sevillano: Colección de artículos publicados en "El Liberal" de Sevilla.* 2 vols. Sevilla: F. Díaz, 1917. Includes

the story of Coloma's near fatal wound (2:113–22), which, according to
the author, resulted from "a question of skirts" in Seville. Pages 51–58
also directly concern Coloma.

Cejador y Frauca, Julio. *Historia de la lengua y literatura castellana.* Madrid:
Tip. de la Revista de Archivos, 1918. 9:393–98. Cejador, himself a former Jesuit, writes about Coloma and *Pequeñeces.* Says Coloma wrote his
first novelistic stories in the fashion of Fernán Caballero, "without her
tenderness of feeling, rather with the dryness characterizing Jesuit writers." His language is "incorrect and even cacophonic, but picturesque
and lively." Adds a bibliographical essay quoting the criticism of Federico
Balart and Emilia Pardo Bazán.

———. *Mirando a Loyola, el alma de la Compañía de Jesús: Novela.* Madrid:
Renacimiento, 1913. Defends the thesis of Ramón Pérez de Ayala en
AMDG. Cejador offers this opinion of Coloma and the Jesuits: "Father
Coloma was born to be a writer, and his entrance into the company
spoiled that, for that's what I consider the vigorous oak tree to be, which
gives only one good acorn and some tiny little ones, the others falling
before their time. . . . If there was anything the Jesuits might distinguish themselves in today, it would be as men of letters. In Spain there
is no one who delves into classical studies as much as they. They are the
only ones who study Greek and Latin practically, translating the authors
and writing and even speaking in these languages. This firm grounding
in humanistic studies should be the starting point of extensive literary
culture; however, the construction stops right there without going one
inch more. Because you can't deny this, that outside of Father Coloma,
there isn't a Spanish Jesuit who knows how to write with his own literary
style. Take the magazine *Razón y Fe,* where you'll find those who know
the most and write the best. If you come up with one sole article, without
your drowsy eyelids closing from the boredom and tastelessness of the
language, then I'll give up" (229–30).

Del Río, Angel. *Historia de la literatura española.* Rev. ed. New York: Holt,
Rinehart, 1963, 219. Contains this succinct statement: "Father Coloma
became for the moment one of the most passionately discussed of authors,
because of the crudeness, bordering on that of the naturalists, with which
he described the libertinism of Madrid aristocracy in his novel *Pequeñeces*
(1890). This is an artistically weak work in which the naturalism ill suits
its end and its moralizing tone; it is only read today as a curiosity and as
an example of the cares of that period."

Dendle, Brian J. "Blasco Ibáñez and Coloma's *Pequeñeces.*" *Romance Notes* 8
(1967):200–203. Argues that in *La araña negra* and *El casamiento de
María,* Blasco Ibáñez answers the thesis novel of Coloma. Discusses the
Restoration politics of *barrer para adentro.*

———. *The Spanish Novel of Religious Thesis, 1876–1936.* Madrid: Editorial

Castalia, 1968. The most complete study of the *novela de tesis*. Contains a long bibliography.

Eguía Ruiz, Constancio. "El P. Luis Coloma. Su vocación literaria." In *Literaturas y literatos*. Barcelona: Librería Religiosa, 1917, 73–197. An encomiastic criticism of Coloma, the "missionary poet," by a fellow Jesuit. Sees a close relationship between moral beauty and artistic beauty.

Estepa, Francisco de. *Los jesuitas y el padre Mir: Cartas a un académico de la Española*. Madrid: La España Editorial, 1896. A two-hundred-page criticism ridiculing Miguel Mir's *Los jesuitas de puertas adentro*. The author says that his "task of scraping away the grammatical mud-splashing from the grimy book of a member of that academy which cleanses and trims the beautiful Castilian language is a work as meritorious as that of curing a leper. . . ." Estepa is the pseudonym of Teodomiro Moreno Durán.

Figueroa, Marqués de. "La novela aristocrática." *La España Moderna* 3 (1891):53–65. Defends Coloma against the charge of writing a *novela de clave*. Argues that *Pequeñeces* is the best of all the "aristocratic novels" in modern Spanish literature. Compares Coloma to Alphonse Daudet.

Flynn, Gerard. "*Pequeñeces*: Novel or Pulpit?" *Revista de Estudios Hispánicos*, 19 (1985):87–96. Concludes that Coloma the novelist does not always practice what Coloma the missionary preaches, and so he lives up to the norm of Horace's *dulcis et utile*.

Gabriel y Ramírez de Cartagena, Alejandro de. "Aportación a un centenario. Seis cartas inéditas del P. Coloma." *Revista Bibliográfica y Documental* 5 (1951):229–39. Contains a bibliography of the "principal editions" of Coloma's works, six of his letters to close friends, and an extraordinary epilogue concerning the near fatal wound he received as a youth.

García Carraffa, Alberto y Arturo. *El Padre Coloma*. Madrid: Imprenta de Juan Pueyo, 1918. An encomiastic biography of Coloma. Contains many anecdotes and pages culled from other authors.

González-Blanco, Andrés. *Historia de la novela en España desde el romanticismo a nuestros días*. Madrid: Sáenz de Jubera, 1909. Sees Coloma as the most outstanding minor novelist of his day. Applies an interesting statement of De Maupassant's *Confession* to Coloma: he is one of those men who "infallibly become in time either saints or nihilists, in whose brains certain ideas exercise an absolute power, whose beliefs are inflexible and whose resolutions unbreakable."

Herrera y Oria, Luis. "*Boy*." *Razón y Fe* 27 (June 1910):212–16. An encomiastic review of *Boy*.

Herrero, Javier. "El testimonio del Padre Coloma sobre Fernán Caballero." *Bulletin of Hispanic Studies* 41 (1964):40–50. Examines various episodes in Coloma's *Recuerdos de Fernán Caballero* (the painting by Madrazo, the conversion of Cecilia's father, the dance held for Wellington, the death of the young liberal conspirator "Leopoldo," the manuscript given to

Washington Irving, the journey to Paris, the publication of *La gaviota*) and concludes that it is evident on every count that Coloma's *Recuerdos,* which "had been generally considered the richest source of biographical information concerning Cecilia Böhl de Faber, is completely lacking in historical value." Coloma is writing *historietas* (fanciful stories) rather than biography.

Hornedo, Rafael María de. "El escándalo de *Pequeñeces* en el centenario del P. Luis Coloma (1851–1951)." *Razón y Fe* 144 (1951):448–62. Discusses in detail the furious polemic waged over *Pequeñeces.* Quotes many letters and newspaper articles. Defends Coloma.

————. "Ideas del padre Coloma sobre la novela." *Razón y Fe* 161 (1960):245-56. Traces the ideas of Coloma on the novel, which ranged from excessive moralization as a young man to a balance of *arte docente* and *arte por el arte* as an older author. Discusses the theories of Fernán Caballero, Gertrudis de Avellaneda, Pereda, and Galdós.

————. "Menéndez Pelayo y el padre Coloma." *Razón y Fe* 103 (1956):759–72. Presents an interesting problem. In his writings, the great critic Menéndez Pelayo makes no judgment or criticism of Coloma, and in his papers there is no letter from Coloma. On the other hand, in Coloma's papers there are two letters from Menéndez Pelayo. The author also examines letters between Menéndez Pelayo and Pereda, and between Coloma and Pereda. Conclusion: Menéndez Pelayo's opinion of Coloma's works was positive though not enthusiastic. The reader senses that something was awry in the relationship of Menéndez Pelayo and Coloma; for example, the former did not attend Coloma's reception into the Royal Academy on 6 December 1908 although he attended the regular meeting of 10 December.

Hoyos y Vinent, Antonio de. *El primer estado (Actuación de la aristocracia antes de la revolución, en la revolución y después de ella).* Madrid: Renacimiento, 1931, 13, 48, 153–58. Coloma asked Hoyos y Vinent, when the latter was a young author, to finish *Boy* for him. Hoyos y Vinent describes the offer, and his reaction to it.

Kempis, Thomas à. *The Imitation of Christ.* Edited by Harold C. Gardiner, S. J. Garden City: Hanover House, 1955. A modern version based on the English translation, made by Richard Whitford around the year 1530. Kempis's *Imitation* was the favorite reading of Luis Coloma.

Lema, Marqués de. *Mis recuerdos (1880–1901).* Madrid: Compañía Ibero-Americana, 1930. The memoirs of a famous statesman. Pages 83–84 concern the duchess of Villahermosa, Coloma, and his *Retratos de antaño.*

Linares Rivas, Manuel. *Boy.* Madrid: Sáez Hermanos, 1929. Adaptation of Coloma's *Boy* to the stage, by a famous dramatist. Unlike the novel, the play has a happy ending.

López-Morillas, Juan. "La Revolución de Septiembre y la novela española." *Revista de Occidente.* 67 (1968):94–115. Discusses the Revolution of 1868 and its relation to the Spanish novel. This volume of *Revista de Occidente* is devoted to the Revolution of 1868.

Martínez Barrionuevo, M. *Un libro funesto (Pequeñeces del P. Coloma).* Barcelona: Librería de López, 1891. This book, a series of articles the author published in 1891, argues that *Pequeñeces* must be studied from the viewpoint of the moral order, the sociopolitical order, and the literary order. Morally, Coloma fails to move the reader, for his sinful character, Currita Albornoz, is more attractive than the virtuous characters. Politically, the novel strikes Martínez Barrionuevo as the Jesuits' abandonment of the Alphonsine party in Spain. As literature, *Pequeñeces* would not be read were it not for the political diatribe. Coloma's book turns out to be the opposite of what he says it is in his prologue.

Mignet, François Auguste Marie. *The History of Mary, Queen of Scots.* 7th ed. London: Richard Bentley, 1887. Mignet is successful in his attempt to write "with the calm impartiality of history." Neither "the apologist nor the traducer" of Mary, he shows the complex relations of Scotland with England and France prior to Mary's birth, the added religious problems of the sixteenth century, and the virtues and defects of Mary's own character. A comparison of Mignet's masterpiece with *The Martyr Queen* will show that Coloma is more of a popular apologist than a historian. Coloma gathered some of his material from Mignet (See chapter 19 of *The Martyr Queen,* and the prologue to Coloma's *Boy* (Mexico City: Ed. Porrúa, 1966), xxiv.

Mir, Miguel. *Harmonía entre la ciencia y la fe.* Rev. ed. Madrid: Sáenz de Jubera, 1892. Proposes to show the harmony of science and faith, in answer to John William Draper's *Historia de los conflictos entre la religión y la ciencia.*

————. *Historia interna documentada de la Compañía de Jesús.* 2 vols. Madrid: Jaime Rates Martín, 1913. The author, a Jesuit for thirty-four years, spent thirty years editing the letters of St. Ignatius of Loyola and studying the history of the Jesuits. These two volumes, which take a dim view of the Jesuit order, are a result of his labors. The life of Miguel Mir (1841–1912) stands in contrast to that of Luis Coloma (1851–1915). The former fought with his superiors, did not let them limit his work, and left the Jesuit order in 1891. Coloma, on grounds of obedience, permitted his superiors to interrupt his work on *Boy* for some fifteen years. Both men were members of the Royal Academy.

————. *Los jesuitas de puertas adentro, o, Un barrido hacia afuera en la Compañía de Jesús.* Barcelona: Luis Tasso, 1896. Father Mir argues that: (1) the Jesuits do not practice humility and do not really follow the rule of St. Ignatius; (2) the power of the order is concentrated in the hands of a few mediocre men who lack spontaneity and rule through an excessive amount of legislation; (3) the Jesuits are a source of quarrels and disorder; (4) the Jesuits are avid readers of newspapers, which strangely govern their lives, rather than the works of scholars and scientists; (5) that as late as 1868, the year of revolution, almost no Jesuits left the order in Spain, whereas by 1896 many were leaving. Curiously, Mir left the Jesuits in the same year that saw the publication of *Pequeñeces,* which he refers to unfavorably on pages 12 and 33; moreover, the title of this book with its *puertas adentro* and *barrido hacia afuera* seems to be a play on words of the Restoration, *barrer para adentro,* a concept scorned by Coloma in his novel.

Muiños Sáenz, Conrado. *Horas de vacaciones: Cuentos morales para los niños.* 1885. 3d ed. Madrid: Imprenta de Luis Aguado, 1897. These stories, written to edify children, resemble Coloma's *Lecturas recreativas.*

Palau, Melchor de. *Acontecimientos literarios, 1889.* Madrid: V. Velázquez, 1890, 42–49. Discusses *Juan Miseria* and *Por un piojo.* The author rejects Coloma's theory of the novel but says he is one of the best contemporary Spanish novelists. Says Coloma shares one defect with Fernán Caballero: "he shows his cards at the beginning of the game, to the prejudice of interest in the novel."

―――. *Acontecimientos literarios, 1890.* Madrid: Librería de D. A. San Martín, 1891, 18–32. Discusses *Pequeñeces.* Palau says that Coloma has thrown off the babyish strollers which delighted the readers of *The Messenger of the Sacred Heart.* Argues that *Pequeñeces* is not a *roman à clef.* Coloma's morality of *aislamiento* and *fumigación* (isolation and fumigation) is not practicable.

Pardo Bazán, Emilia. *El P. Luis Coloma: Biografía y estudio crítico.* Madrid: Sáenz de Jubera, 1891. This book appeared shortly after the publication of *Pequeñeces,* "a work of bloody and burning satire." Argues that Coloma knew the aristocratic world from *within* and that his data are exact *in themselves*; "only that, carefully grouped, placed in a certain light and relief, they produce a pejorative effect, they make high society uglier than it really is if we consider it in its entirety, a mixture of some of the good, a lot of the bad and a whole lot of indifference and banality." Argues that the true subject of *Pequeñeces* is the Restoration, which Coloma sees as "a Turkish warship with a Christian flag." Doña Emilia Pardo Bazán was a marchioness and one of Spain's most distinguished novelists.

―――. "Polémica: A Fray Conrado Muiños Sáenz, Agustiniano." In *Nuevo Teatro Crítico.* Madrid: La España Editorial, Junio 1891, 19–33. A famous novelist answers a critic who had taken exception to her own criticism of Coloma and *Bagatelles.* She writes about Coloma, Pereda, and Galdós, tendentious literature in general, and "that *haine de la littérature* that affects us so."

Pereda, José María de. *Epistolario de Pereda y Menéndez Pelayo*: Preface and notes by María Fernanda de Pereda y Torres Quevedo and Enrique Sánchez Reyes. Santander: Hermanos Bedia, 1953. In letters 74 and 76–78 (all of the year 1888) Coloma, via Pereda, asks a favor of Menéndez Pelayo. Both Menéndez Pelayo and Pereda discuss the latter's novel about the aristocracy, *La Montálvez*. These letters bear out Padre Hornedo's contention that Menéndez Pelayo never wrote about Coloma's literature.

Pérez de Ayala, Ramón. *A.M.D.G.* Madrid: Renacimiento, 1910. In this thesis novel a famous author answers Coloma's thesis in *Pequeñeces.* Pérez de Ayala despises the Jesuits.

Pérez Clotet, Pedro. *Algunas notas sobre la Andalucía del P. Coloma.* Cádiz: Imprenta de Salvador Repeto, 1940. An address given at Jerez de la Frontera in 1938. Discusses the Andalusian quality of Coloma's works, comparing him with Fernán Caballero and Pedro Antonio de Alarcón. The author has an antirevolutionary bias.

Peseux-Richard, H. *"Pequeñeces . . . por el P. Luis Coloma." Revue Hispanique* 1 (1894):92–94. A favorable review of the fifth edition of *Pequeñeces* (Bilbao, 1891). Calls Coloma a "Savonarola who knew how to adapt himself to the exigencies of his day." Cites errors in Coloma's use of foreign words.

Pidal y Mon, Alejandro. *Discursos leídos ante la Real Academia Española en la recepción pública del Rvdo: P. Luis Coloma el día 6 de diciembre de 1908.* Madrid: Revista de Arch., Bibl. y Museos, 1908. Contains two speeches, Coloma's address to the Royal Academy on his becoming a member, and the reply of his fellow academician, Alejandro Pidal y Mon, whose prose reflects the ornate, complicated style fashionable among nineteenth-century authors.

Ragucci, Rodolfo. *Letras castellanas: Lecciones de historia literaria española.* Rosario: Editorial Apis, 1941, 527–29. Information about Coloma.

Risco, Alberto. *Cisneros.* Mexico City: Editorial Latino-America, 1943. Risco's book appears as the "Libro Segundo" or continuation of Coloma's *Fray Francisco* and is bound together with it in one volume.

Ruiz Amado, Ramón, S. J. *Don Miguel Mir y su historia documentada de la Compañía de Jesús: Estudio crítico.* Barcelona: Librería Religiosa, 1914. A refutation of Mir's criticism of the Jesuits. Accuses Mir of rhetoric rather than scholarship.

———. *"Jeromín." Razón y Fe* 19 (1907):110–12. An encomiastic review of Coloma's *Jeromín.*

Schmid, Christoph von. *Cuentos de Schmid.* 2d ed. Barcelona: Casa Editorial Araluce, 1932. The exemplary stories of Canon Schmid (1768–1854) were translated from German into several languages. Coloma's *Lecturas recreativas* fall within their tradition.

Schumacher, John N. "Integrism: A Study in Nineteenth Century Spanish Politico-Religious Thought." *Catholic Historical Review* 48 (1962):343–64. Discusses the position of the Liberals, the Liberal-Conservatives, the Traditionalists, the Carlists, and the Integrists in Spain from 1868 to

1905. It was especially on the Jesuits that Ramón Nocedal and the Integrists, the most conservative group of all, "relied for . . . support and advice." But after 1892 the Jesuits began to break away from Nocedal, and the final blow came with their desertion in 1905. From this article, one gathers that Coloma wrote *Pequeñeces* (1890) in the midst of some profound changes within the church and the Jesuit order in Spain. His thought ("the altar and the throne") seems to be generally Traditionalist, though not specifically Carlist or Integrist. He looked to Isabel II as his queen and her son Alfonso as her rightful heir, but he was (like the Carlists and Integrists) disgusted with the Restoration government of Spain.

Suárez Bravo, Ceferino. *España demagógica.* Madrid: Imprenta de Dubrull, 1873. A reading of Suárez Bravo will show that many of Coloma's expressions must have come from a common conservative rhetoric, for example, *fango, lodo, fondos cenagosos* (see Suárez Bravo, 9-10, 81, 162). His attitude toward revolution resembles Coloma's: "There is nothing that seduces the public like novelty. That's why those who stir up the social mud (*fango*) show so much zeal in making people believe that all modern revolutions come pregnant with some new thing. The novelty of the thing, which is always the same, dates, however, from a date prior to history, to the world, to the ages, and even to time itself. In the first revolutionary flag raised between heaven and the abyss by Lucifer, there was already written with letters of fire this novelty, reduced to these two words: *Non serviam*; that is to say, *we will not obey,* or, what's the same, *we will to rule.* Whoever cannot see in these words the essence of the program of all contemporary rebellions, is lacking eyes in his intellect" (9–10). Suárez Bravo also speaks of the Masons (159).

Valera, Juan. *Correspondencia de don Juan Valera (1859–1905).* Edited, with introduction, by Cyrus C. De Coster. Madrid: Editorial Castalia, 1956. The letters on pages 162–65 and 248–50 throw light on Valera's attitude towards Coloma.

———. "*Pequeñeces.* Currita Albornoz, al Padre Luis Coloma." In *Obras completas,* vol 2. Madrid: Aguilar, 1961, 841–56. The great novelist, Valera, pretending to be Currita Albornoz of *Pequeñeces,* writes Coloma an ironical letter objecting to his bitter satire, implacable morality, and harshness in the style of Jansen and Calvin. At the end *she* protests that although autumnal she is still very beautiful!

Vega, Fernando de la. "El Padre Coloma." *Cuba Contemporánea* 22 (1920):91–98. A brief description of Coloma's life and works. Compares *Pequeñeces* to the *novelas de tesis* of Galdós and Alarcón. Says Coloma writes his biographies "with a magnifying glass."

Wast, Hugo (pen name of Gustavo A. Martínez Zuviría). *Confidencias de un novelista.* Buenos Aires: Editores de Hugo Wast, 1931. An Argentine novelist presents his theory of the novel. Part 4, which concerns "Morality in Art and Especially in the Novel," dedicates three pages of approval to *Pequeñeces* (158–60).

Weingarten, Barry E. "La pervivencia del folletín: *Pequeñeces* del Padre Coloma." *Explicación de Textos Literarios* 13 (1984–85):67–75. Argues that Coloma's thesis novel of 1891 hearkens back to the serial novels of 1840–70 rather than to new trends in novel writing. Thus *Pequeñeces*, written in defense of Spanish traditionalism, is retrograde, "without anything new whatsoever."

Index